SOLDIERS
OF
DESTRUCTION

TEXAS IS THE REASON

THE MAVERICKS OF LONE STAR PUNK

PHOTOGRAPHY BY PAT BLASHILL

WORDS BY RICHARD LINKLATER • DAVID YOW

ADRIANE "ASH" SHOWN • DONNA RICH • TERESA TAYLOR

Bazillion Points

FOR EVERYONE WHO WAS THERE

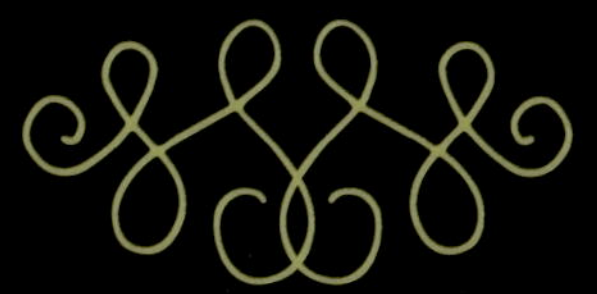

THE BIG BOYS

THE DICKS

BUTT HOLE SURFERS

THURSDAY, May 27th
AT THE BONHAM EXCHANGE
1.00 TO GET IN CLUB. 2.00
TO THRASH. CLUB admission
FREE WITH COLLEGE I.D.
MUSIC AT 9:20.
35¢ BEER 75¢ HIGH BALLS

The Mavericks of Lone Star Punk
by Pat Blashill

Second printing, published 2021 by

Bazillion Points
Callicoon | New York | U.S.A.
WWW.BAZILLIONPOINTS.COM
@BAZILLIONPOINTS

Produced for Bazillion Points by Ian Christe
Layout and design by Bazillion Points

A bazillion thank-yous to Michael Azerrad, King Coffey, Polly Watson, Phil Wilhelm, Chris Anderson, Vivi, Roman, Dianna, the Hornbahn, and the Western Hotel.

Library of Congress Control Number: 2019949055
Library of Congress Cataloging-in-Publication Data is available upon request.

ISBN 978-1-935950-17-2

Printed in China

Title overleaf: **The Offenders**, Voltaire's Basement, June 1984.
Dedication: **David Yow of Scratch Acid**, Uncle Sue Sue's, July 1984.

Contents

W. E. MOORE
11308

"Texas...is a mystique closely approximating a religion... People either passionately love Texas or passionately hate it, and, as in other religions, few people dare to inspect it for fear of losing their bearings in mystery or paradox."—**John Steinbeck**, ***Travels with Charley***

Suburban Home, December 1985.

Previous: **Hurlbut Ranch**, Dripping Springs, Texas, June 1985.

Honky-tonk Marquee, Braker Lane, Austin, 1979.

Facing: **Hill Country Bar**, Granger, Texas, May 1986; **Lynda Stuart and Renee Miller**, Liberty Lunch, Summer 1984.

ROCK
CULT
FILTH

John "Control Rat X" Slate, Adriane "Ash" Shown, and Buxf Parrot, Uncle Sue Sue's, June 1984.

Facing: **Flag-Bearers** and **Youth Band**, 1984 Republican National Convention, Dallas, August 1984.

Next: **Delegate Prayer**, 1984 Republican National Convention, Dallas, August 1984.

SOUTH CAROLINA
DELEGATE
DELEGATE
DELEGATE
BUSH

YLVANIA
REAGAN BUSH

NOW
K.K.K P.O. 3324
PASADENA TEXAS 77501

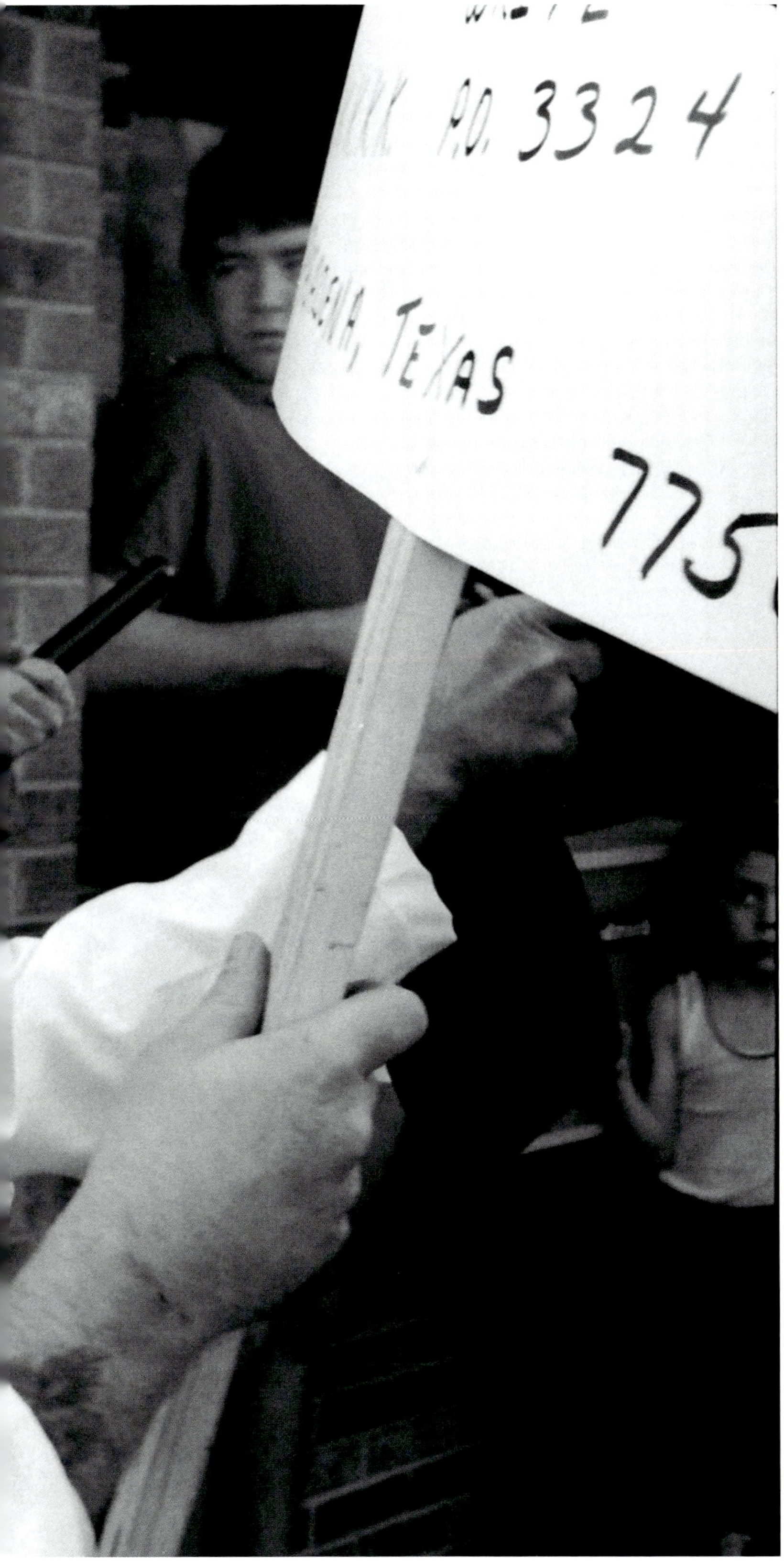

"*Mayor Carole McClellan said Sunday police will conduct an investigation into alleged police brutality against a Hispanic activist beaten during a violence-plagued Ku Klux Klan march.*" **–United Press International, *February 20, 1983***

Ku Klux Klan rally,
Texas State Capital, February 19, 1983.

Next: **Ku Klux Klan rally**,
Texas State Capital, February 19, 1983.

After: **Chris and Mike's Backyard**, Spring 1984.

RCA

WE WERE THERE

BY RICHARD LINKLATER

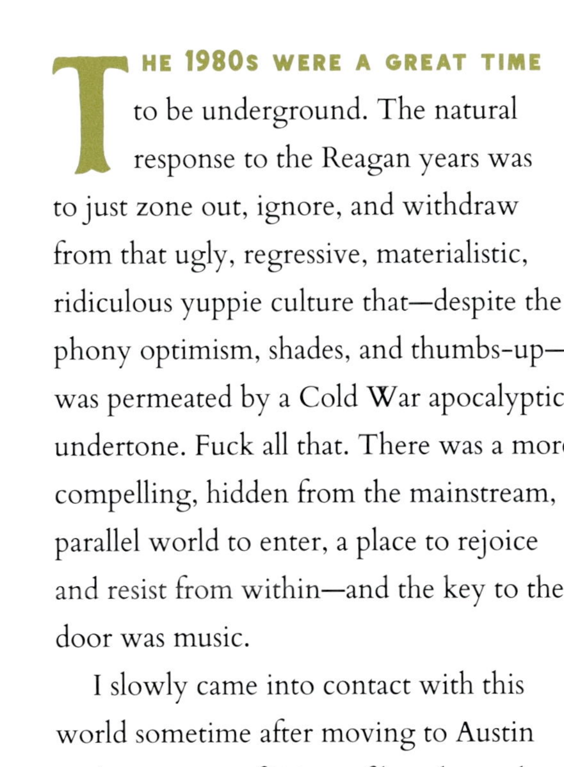

THE 1980s WERE A GREAT TIME to be underground. The natural response to the Reagan years was to just zone out, ignore, and withdraw from that ugly, regressive, materialistic, ridiculous yuppie culture that—despite the phony optimism, shades, and thumbs-up—was permeated by a Cold War apocalyptic undertone. Fuck all that. There was a more compelling, hidden from the mainstream, parallel world to enter, a place to rejoice and resist from within—and the key to the door was music.

I slowly came into contact with this world sometime after moving to Austin in the summer of '83 as a film-obsessed college dropout and laid-off offshore oil worker. It seemed like everyone I was meeting was either some combination of musician, painter, writer, photographer, actor, and filmmaker, or a cool academic studying and writing about those things. No one asked or cared much about how you paid your rent or what day job you might have held—that didn't mean anything. In this world you were defined by what you were passionate about—your ideas and what you were creating—not how you fit into the economy.

The connective tissue and the air we were all breathing came from the bands and the shows. Holy shit, what a transference of energy! Whether you were at a bigger show surrounded by hundreds of fellow freaks, or at some tiny venue or house party with twenty-five others, your spirit was being fed, and just by being there you became a part of something. If Austin bands made no single overriding sound, their sole musical commonality was probably the lack of anything formulaic; just this wonderful cacophony of uncompromised psychedelic madness, Dadaist absurdity, auditory irreverence, sincerity, and joy. The attitude celebrated in-the-moment expression, completely lacking in pretense, self-importance, and grandiosity. I remember asking a friend if there was a difference between this music scene in Austin and those in other places. "If you hit the ground in the mosh pit here, someone immediately helps you up.

HOUSE PARTY, SUMMER 1983.

In other places they just trample you until you manage to get up on your own." Yes, good ol' tolerant, caring Austin.

Pat Blashill was always a calm presence, fixing his camera at his eye, freezing moments and people in time. Seeing his photos all these years later is a profound experience for me. So many old friends appear, some of them no longer with us. I recognize the faces of people I never knew well, or at all, but who I *liked* all the same and felt kinship with. I remember that gleam in their eyes, the communal passion, and the unspoken acknowledgment that we were all here in this underground by choice, and that there was nowhere else we'd rather be.

Skinhead with Geronimo, East 12th St., January 1985; **Graffiti**, Mexico City, Winter 1984.

Next: **Big Boys Crowd**, RNC protest, August 1984.

DROP DEAD!
DONT
GET
THE

"I'm a redneck fag. It's like, 'You don't like it? Fuck you.'"—**Gary Floyd, the Dicks**

The Dicks, Voltaire's Basement, April 1984.

Next: **Gary Floyd of the Dicks** and **Cristi Delgado**, Voltaire's Basement, April 1984.

Big Boys crowd, Republican National Convention protest, August 1984.

Facing, above: **Continental Club**, March 4, 1984.

Facing, below: **Big Boys crowd**, RNC protest, August 1984.

Front and Center at a Big Boys Show, August 1982.

Facing: **Rey Washam of the Big Boys**, RNC protest, August 1984.

Next: **Randy "Biscuit" Turner**, the Big Boys, Liberty Lunch, September 1984.

"One day, Chris and I decided that we should form a band. We flipped a coin to choose who would play bass. The next day Chris went to Raul's, and he asked the people there, 'What does it take to play here?' And the guy said, 'When do you want to play?'" —**Tim Kerr, Big Boys**

ROLLER
BONES

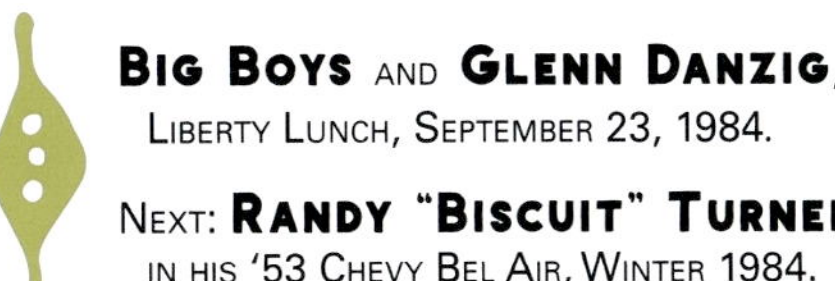

Big Boys and **Glenn Danzig**,
Liberty Lunch, September 23, 1984.

Next: **Randy "Biscuit" Turner**
in his '53 Chevy Bel Air, Winter 1984.

Biscuit at home, Winter 1984.

Facing: **Chris Gates and Mike Carroll's Place**, Fall 1984; **Phillippe's place**, Spring 1984.

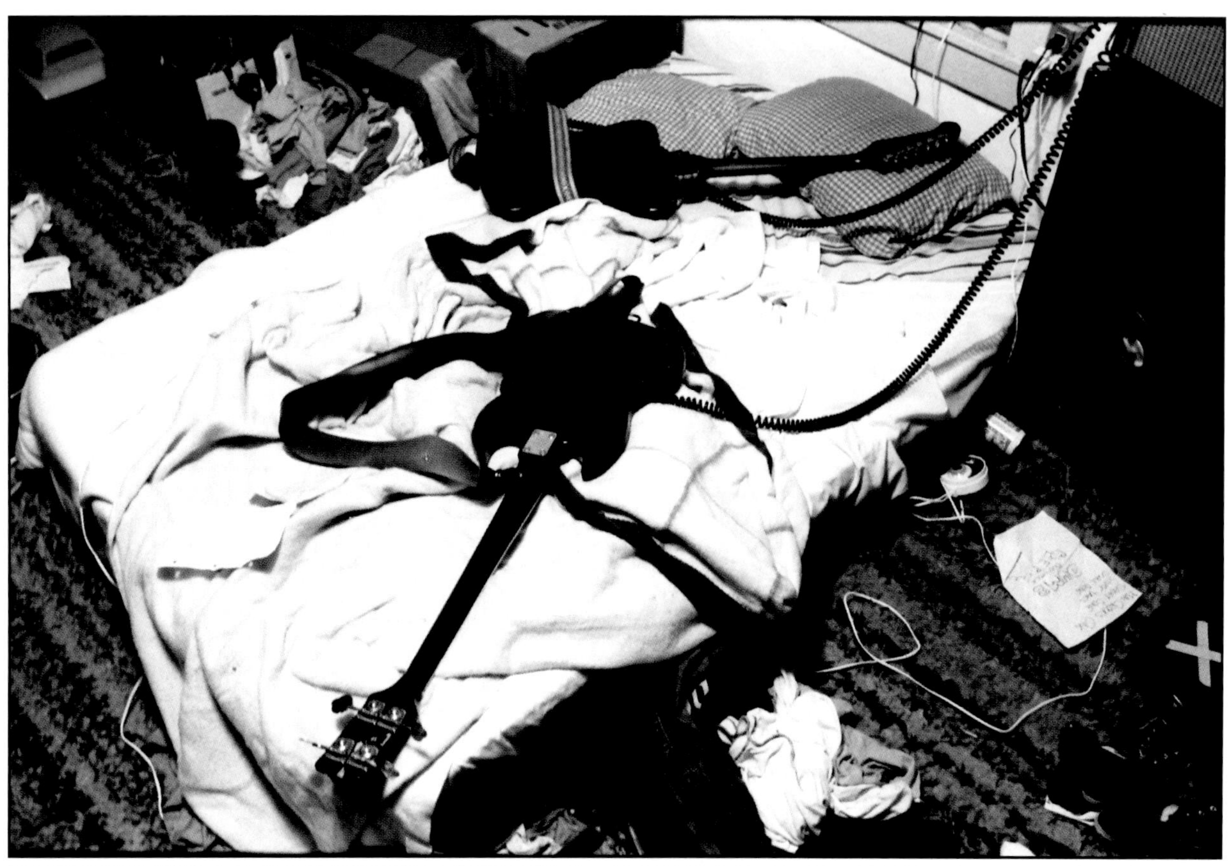

David Yow's Bed, Scratch Acid House, Fall 1982; **My Room**, Halcyon Co-op, Fall 1982.

ABOVE: **MARK "CHICO" MCCULLOUGH** AT A DEAD KENNEDYS SHOW, THE RITZ, AUGUST 1982.

BELOW: **CHRIS GATES AND MIKE CARROLL'S PLACE**, FALL 1984.

Karla Eppler, Halcyon Co-op, September 1982; **Ash**, Fall 1984.

Original Scratch Acid singer **Steve Anderson** and **Space Kitty**, Fall 1982.

Lynda Stuart at her parents' house, Fall 1984.

Chris Wing of Sharon Tate's Baby, Winter 1980; **Dino Lee's Place**, January 1985.

Richard Mather of Criminal Crew, Fall 1984.

Facing: **Lynda Stuart and Rene Miller at Home**, Fall 1984.

Next: **Lynda Stuart** in her room, Fall 1984.

MAN

JAN.21
+more!
KENNEDY
OFFENDERS,
CRIMINAL
Überfall!
F.U
MONDAY
SHOW

THU JULY 12
CONTINENTAL CLUB
G.B.H
FROM ENGLAND
HENCHMEN
death of glory
IMMORAL ATTITUDE
THE LAST NIGHT AT VOLTAIR
MEAT JOY
THUR JULY 19th
G.B.H
WHITE PRIDE
Saturday MARCH 10th
T.S.O.L.
$5
+ peace core
legion of doom
kennedy's
CRIMINAL CREW
SAT. 20th LIBERTY LUNCH
WHAM!
SAT. MAR. 3
NNEDYS
big boys
MAY 25
PRIVATE SECTOR
JUNE 6
PEARL MUSIC HALL
D.R.I.
AT PACKIN HOUSE
TOMORROW
$3
8:30
1984
TASTE OF DENVER
OPEN DEFIANCE
Headbanger presents
MISFITS
EVICTION PARTY
7:00
137
HAPPY WORLD
U.S.A
2011 Glenarm pl.

Phillippe LaVere at Work, KUT-FM, Spring 1984.

THE 1983
Austin Chronicle
MUSIC POLL AWARDS
Ceremony

Texan to the Core

by Donna Rich

I WAS THE FIRST GIRL at McCallum High School in Austin to dress punk. It was very scandalous. My senior year, on the day of the National Honor Society induction ceremony, I wore jeans that I had torn up and put back together with dozens of safety pins. My English teacher came to me, soberly informed me I was going to be in the Honor Society, and asked me to change into something less outrageous. I had no idea that I was even in the running. Fortunately, I already kept a backup outfit handy, because I had been sent home previously for dressing too wild.

As a teen, I read *Creem* and *Rolling Stone*. I don't think I really understood punk, though, until John Slate, aka Control Rat X, started sharing his favorite music with me. We were in Latin class together, and he was the first boy I ever dated. After we became close, he lent me Elvis Costello's *This Year's Model*. I still remember everything that was happening around me later that day when I first played the record. I absolutely loved that music and wanted to hear more. I remember staring at the album cover, dumbfounded and confused by the odd choice of images.

Punk offered something so amazing for a depressed, lost, misfit teen like me. I'm a gentle person, but I was also bullied in school and was raised with some significant emotional deprivation. I didn't have the words for how angry I was about my own life until I heard punk. I loved the furious messages in the music.

Before punk and the music scene, I was very shy and had few friends. I certainly didn't go on dates. I was isolated but not sure how to change it. Punk culture celebrated being different and angry, and, for the first time, I felt empowered. I finally felt okay. Sometimes I even felt beautiful. My French teacher said that the year I found punk I was "like a butterfly," because acting and dressing more boldly changed the way people saw me and how I saw myself.

John Slate introduced me to the Rev. Neil X's new wave and punk radio show

Donna Rich, June 1985.

Rock of the Ages, and soon I discovered everything happening with punk in Austin. My favorite bands included the Dicks, whose lyrics were brave and honest: they criticized the police and talked openly about the sex life of a gay man. The Dicks blew off the top of my head—I was in love.

On my mom's side, I'm a sixth generation Texan, and on my father's, I'm a third generation Texan. I am very proud of that, but at the same time, I have lived with all the racism, sexism, and homophobia baked into Texas culture. Growing up in small Texas towns like Big Spring, I heard adults use racial epithets on a daily basis. This hurt and scared me—sometimes they were attacking my friends.

My aunt Carol helped me and my sister Becky a lot after our parents died. She was gay, and I saw how badly homophobia in West Texas affected her. She died in her early sixties, and I think her life was shortened by the internalized hatred she had faced. I saw how she had to hide who she was and who she loved. It's still infuriating and gut-wrenching that she was made to feel ashamed of her life.

Punks like Gary Floyd of the Dicks and Biscuit of the Big Boys are Texan to the core—they represent the disavowed part of Texas. When you are gay in a small Texas town, I think you hear about places like Austin or Houston, where people are freethinking, and you begin to hope that you can go there and have a better time. That is part of what punk in Austin represented to me—a home where you could be expressive and accepted. Gary and Biscuit expressed themselves freely, and at great risk. They are heroes to me—they showed me how to be authentic and strong.

Despite the rampant drug use and occasional violence surrounding the punk scene, I don't think I ever felt afraid. Some people I certainly thought were strange and should be avoided, like Elbow. I remember seeing him one day outside the Continental Club, talking to a group of young women, proclaiming, "I deserve a blow job. It's my birthday!"

I was more afraid of hateful non-punks, especially frat boys, who often showed themselves to be racist and intolerant. When Richard Mather had a Mohawk, he was attacked and had to be hospitalized; after that, I was very worried for all of us.

The thing that amazed me about punk music in Austin was how creative and passionate everyone was. Most everyone who wasn't a musician either had a zine, took photos, dressed in an interesting and inspiring way, or simply supported and loved the bands. I was excited by how wide open the field was, and how many ways there were to play. I sold clothes that I designed at Dressed to Kill, and worked on a 'zine with Bill Daniel. Later on, Wade Driver and I had our band, Windowpain. When the Big Boys said, "Now go start your own band!" it wasn't just a tagline—the spirit was real.

NEXT: **BUTTHOLE SURFERS** (L-R: TERENCE SMART, GIBBY HAYNES, PAUL LEARY, TERESA TAYLOR, KING COFFEY) WITH **MARK FARNER** (FOREGROUND), AT B.O.S.S. STUDIOS, SAN ANTONIO, JULY 1984.

ABOVE AND FACING: **BUTTHOLE SURFERS**, UNCLE SUE SUE'S, WINTER 1984.

"Pat snuck behind Teresa and I at Uncle Susu's in 1984 and took this. I don't think I have a picture of so many friends in one picture. That was it. That was our life at that point in time." **–KING COFFEY, BUTTHOLE SURFERS**

Next: **Gibby Haynes and Paul Leary.** Butthole Surfers, Uncle Sue Sue's, Winter 1984.

Following: **Teresa Taylor and King Coffey of the Butthole Surfers**, Uncle Sue Sue's, Winter 1984.

Coors

Paul Leary, Kelly Lynn, and El Borracho, Butthole Surfers, Continental Club, March 4, 1984.

Facing: **Roger "El Borracho" Manriquez**, Continental Club, March 4, 1984.

Next: **Paul Leary**, Recording *Rembrandt Pussyhorse* at B.O.S.S. Studios, San Antonio, July 1984.

DUCK
BUTTER

EXIT
MXR

DISAPPointed
dp

BUTTHOLE SURFERS, JUNE 1984.

Butthole Surfers, Winter 1987.

CHICO (FAR LEFT) AND **THE OFFENDERS**, VOLTAIRE'S BASEMENT, JUNE 1984.

The Offenders (L–R: Tony Johnson, J. J. Jacobson, Mikey Donaldson, and Pat Doyle), Spring 1985.

The Offenders, Liberty Lunch, July 1984

The Offenders, Voltaire's Basement, June 1984.

J.J. Jacobson and Tony Johnson, the Offenders, University of Texas Political Rally, Fall 1984.

Next: **The Offenders**, University of Texas Political Rally, Fall 1984.

IF TH
EVE
LEADE

Marshall

Scott Griswold and Richard Mather of Criminal Crew, Fall 1984.

Paul "Martian" Sessums, Criminal Crew, Fall 1984.

"The Buffalo Gals paid $180 per month to live in the front of a warehouse. My room had no windows and no air conditioning, so I took a sledgehammer and knocked a hole in a wall for a fan. I slept on an army cot, and drove my motorcycle right into the warehouse."—**Kathy McCarty, Buffalo Gals/Glass Eye**

Altar, Chris Gates and Mike Carroll's place, Fall 1984.

Ash at Home, September 1984; **Tim Kerr** of the Big Boys at home, September 1984.

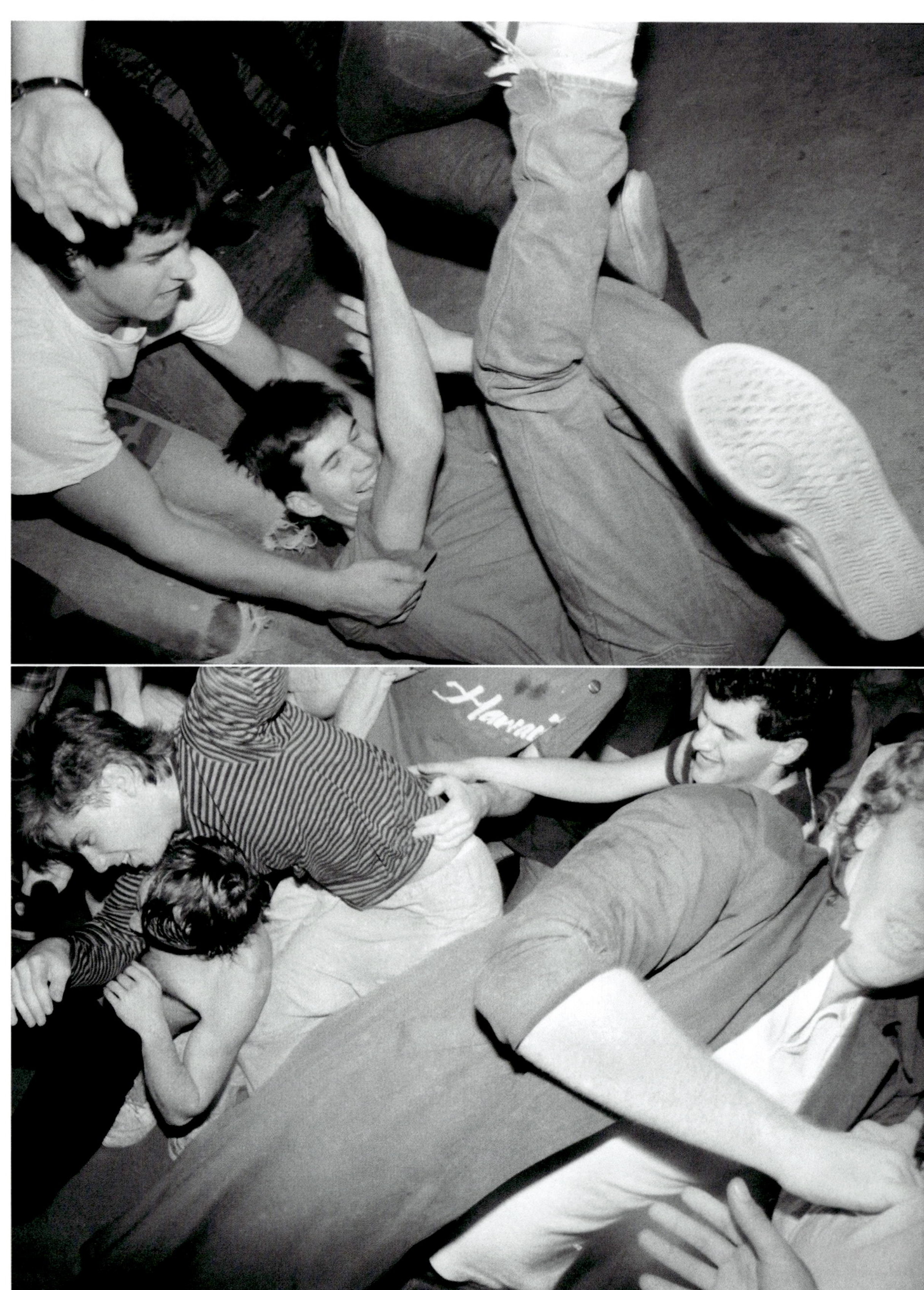

Flipper Show, January 1985; **Garage Party**, February 1985.

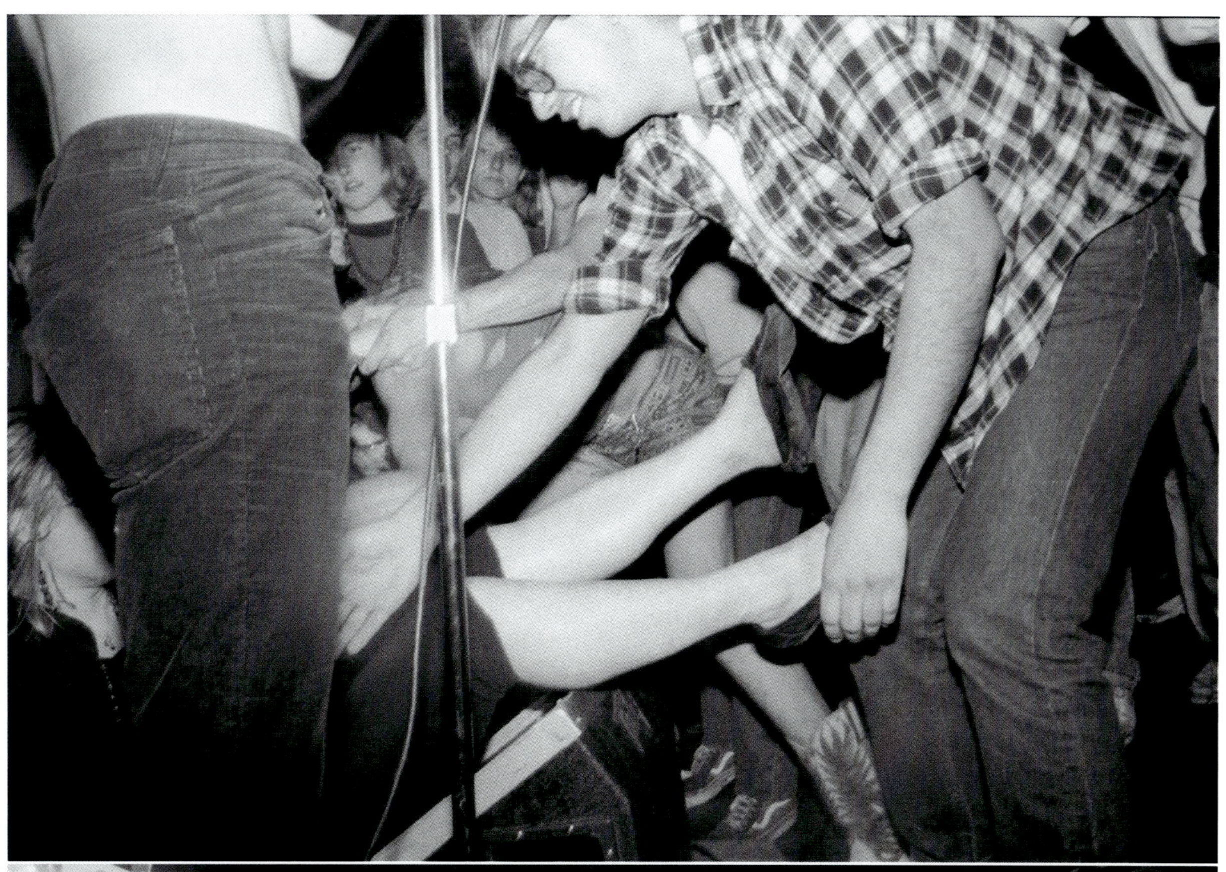

Garage Party, February 1985.

Next: **Poison 13** (From left) Tim Kerr, Mike Carroll, Bill Anderson, Chris Gates, Jim Kanan, Fall 1984.

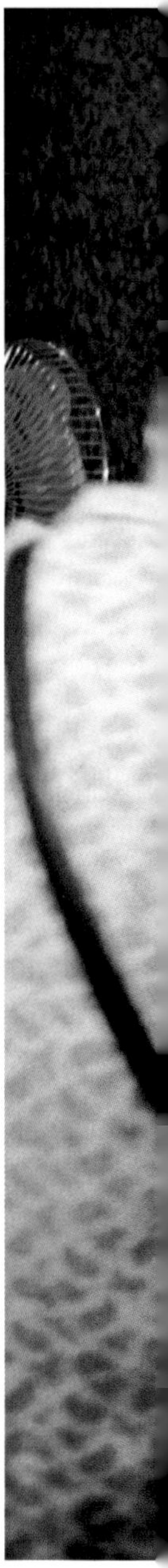

"I think we just wanted to play loud rock songs about drinking, fucking, and killing."—**Bill Anderson, Poison 13**

Poison 13, rehearsal space, Fall 1984.

Mike Carroll of Poison 13, Rollingwood Recording, October 1984.

Facing: **Chris and Bill of Poison 13**, Uncle Sue Sue's, July 1984; **Garage party**, February 1985.

Poison 13
Uncle Sue-Sue's, July 1984.

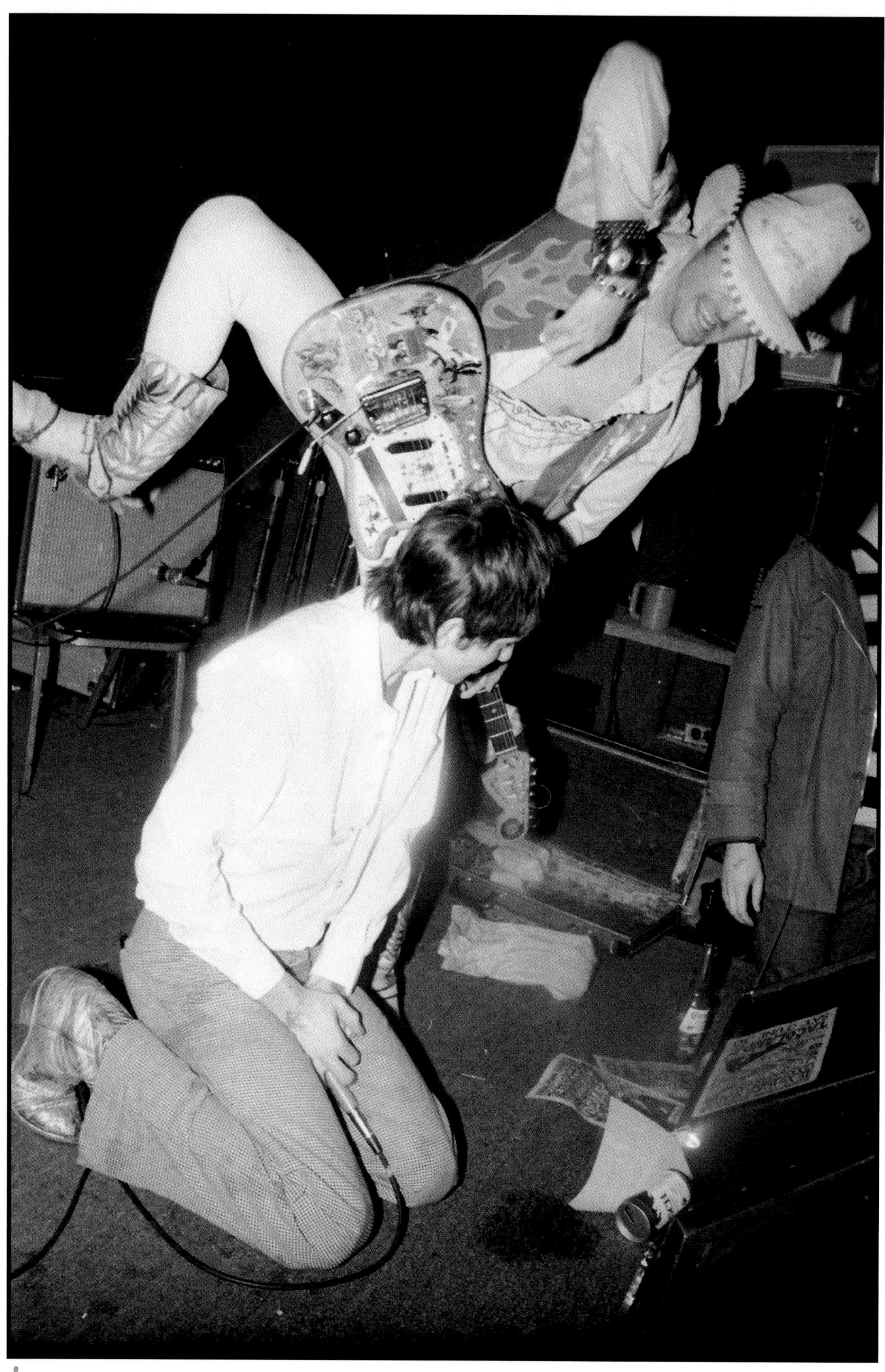

Jeff Smith and Jukebox of the Hickoids, Continental Club, February 1985.

Mike Carroll of Poison 13, Continental Club, February 1985.

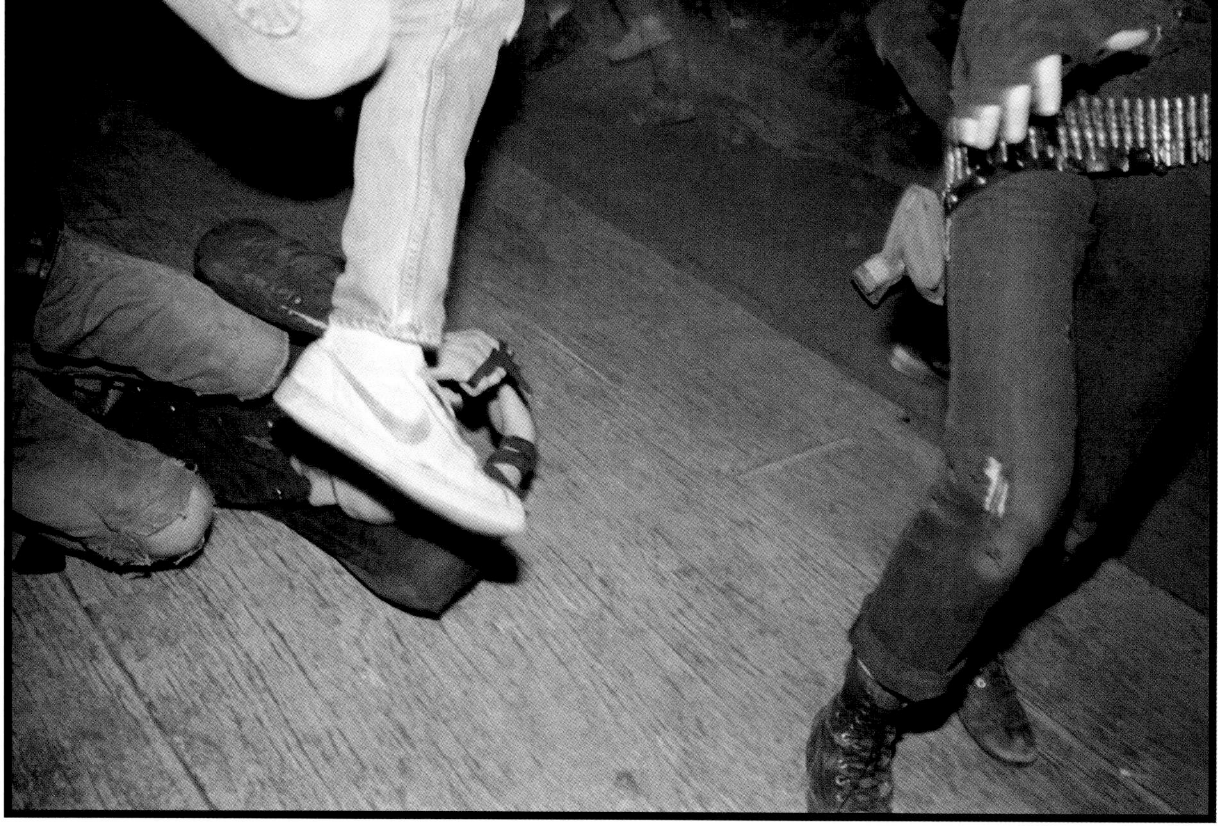

Hopping in, May 1984; **Trampled**, January 1985.

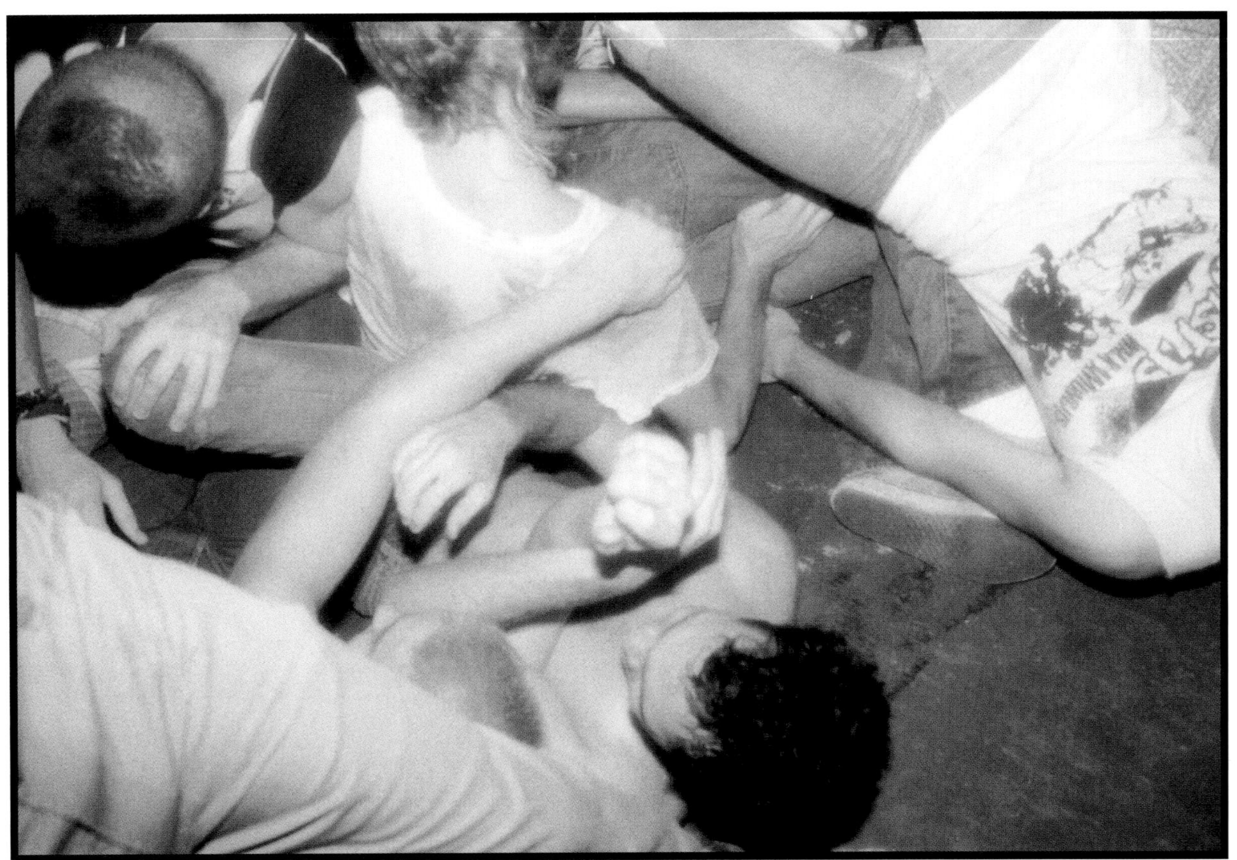

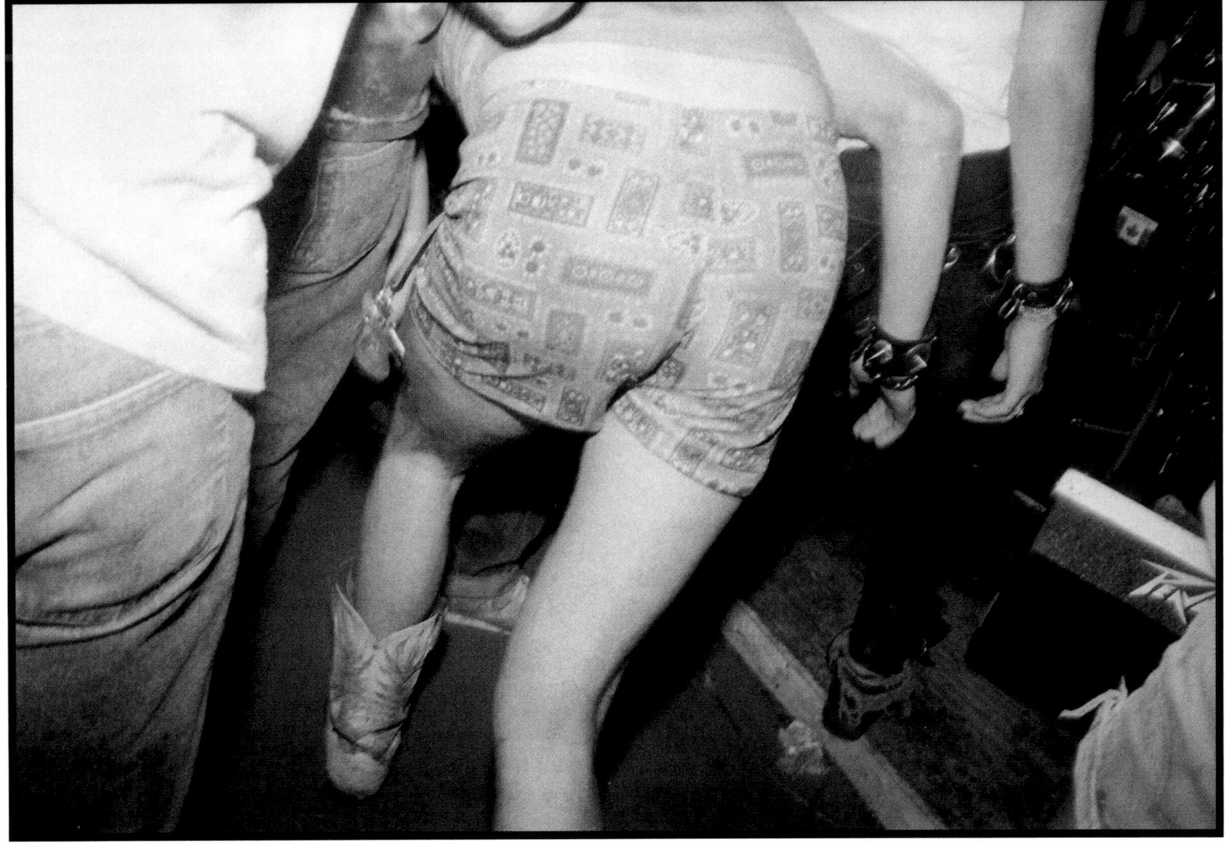

Tangle, August 1984; **Jukebox of the Hickoids**, Spring 1985.

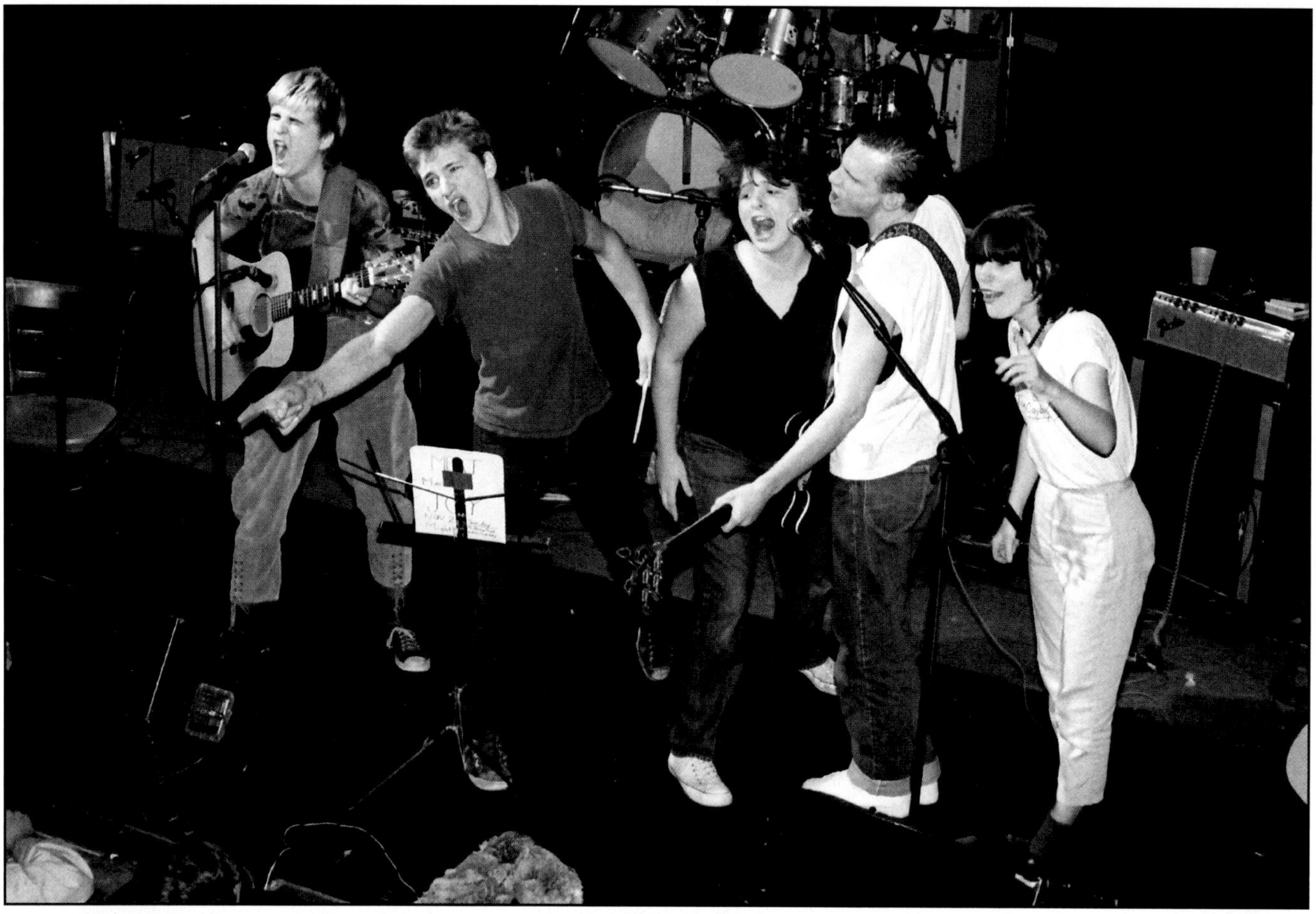

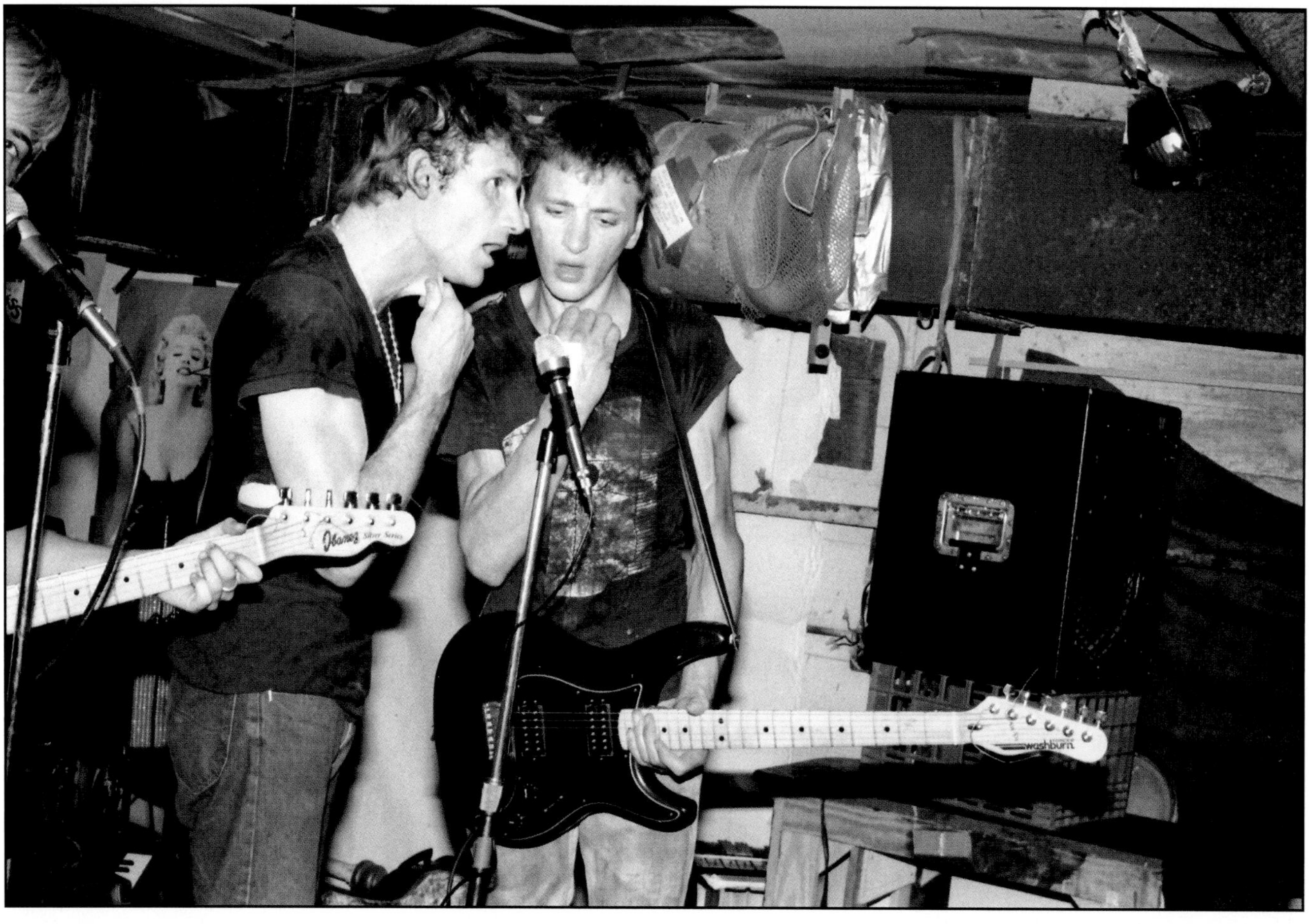
Ibanez Silver Series
washburn

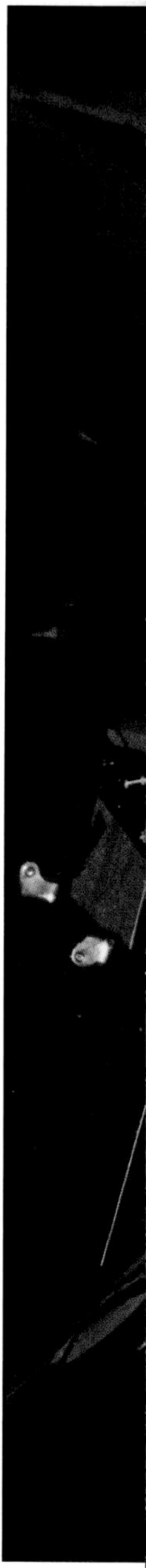

Meat Joy, Club Foot, Fall 1983.

Facing: **Meat Joy** (L–R: Gretchen Phillips, John Perkins, Melissa Cobb, Tim Mateer, and Jamie Spidle), Voltaire's Basement, July 1984; **John Hawkes** (then John Boy Perkins) and **Tim Mateer** of **Meat Joy**, Voltaire's Basement, July 1984.

Next: **Meat Joy**, Voltaire's Basement Final Night, July 1984.

VoLTAIRE
'S BEEN SWE
NG, GAN

Scratch
meat
all of this
4~U!
WHERE'S THE PARTY??!!
HAPPINESS
125

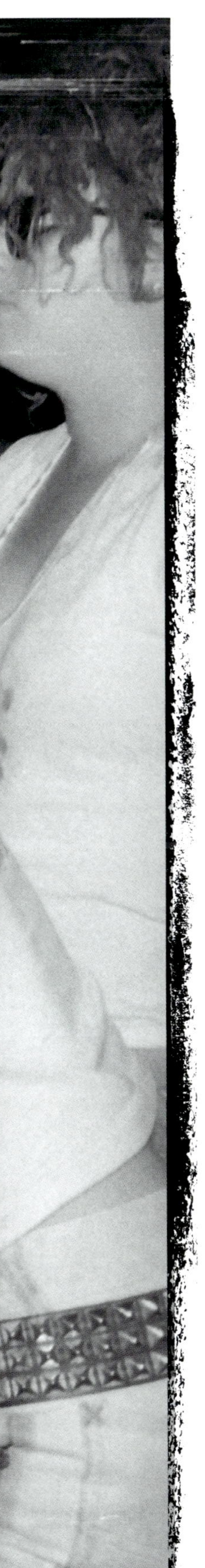

LIFT AS YOU CLIMB

BY ADRIANE "ASH" SHOWN

I WAS A PUNK ROCK DEN MOTHER during the mid-'80s in Austin. I started booking ob-gyn appointments and escorting a small circle of teen girls to the People's Community Clinic for their first exams. They'd say, "We're just *talking* about sex." My response? "If you don't actually learn about sex and your body, you'll just be *talking* about being pregnant."

My troop of girls was twelve-to-fifteen years old, and I wasn't even twenty yet. I had barely known anything at their age. But my hope was that these young women would gain a sense of ownership, and a sense of self. I wanted to see them be truly empowered with knowledge, or at least form a connection to their own anatomy.

After I turned eleven, I got boobs and began to receive a great deal of unwelcome attention from boys and men. I was grabbed and groped by strangers in the street, on the subway on my way to school, by school classmates, by family friends, and by a few dads in the neighborhood. This treatment followed me through high school and young adulthood (and continues to this day—aged auntie that I am). Growing up, a lot of gals gave me grief when I garnered any attention. I doubt they understood that it was nearly all negative.

Then I learned that some men can't help but *try* to put an outspoken woman back in her place. In 1980s Texas, having short pink hair or a tattoo counted as being outspoken, and I had both. I had started going to punk shows at age fourteen in Washington, D.C. But deep in the heart of Texas a few years later, just when I needed them, many young women were taking their places onstage. In the Austin music scene, I found a solid sense of belonging and a sense of safety in the number of other "others."

And the *music*. We had some incredible bands. We knew Austin was quite special then, and every visiting vanload of

ADRIANE "ASH" SHOWN, SONIC YOUTH SHOW, CONTINENTAL CLUB, AUGUST 1985.

musicians could see it, too. Beyond the bands, our fanzines showcased an amazing array of talented writers, poets, visual artists, cartoonists, and photographers. We were called "art fags," but we wore the epithet as a badge of honor.

By the time I turned eighteen, and was regularly going to punk shows in San Antonio and Austin, years of harrassment and abuse had fueled my wrath at anyone who dared to grab me. If I saw another gal being pawed, I intervened the way I wished another gal would have done for me. I took it upon myself to play deputy. I'd pin the guilty party to the wall, and calmly and firmly explain that his behavior would not be tolerated: "Who the fuck do you think you are?! Keep your hands to yourself and I'll do the same."

Maybe I'd tear their T-shirt down the front for emphasis. On occasion, I would grab their crotch in retaliation. And that was usually the end of it. I made room for a few more gals to happily join the mosh pit, unmolested. The rules were pretty simple: No shoving from the sidelines, no sharpened spikes, no grabbing girls.

We all grew up hearing that boys will be boys. But it was unthinkable that guys from the punk scene would ever follow in the misogynistic footsteps of the establishment we railed against. We had our "Summer of Love" turning point at the 1985 Woodshock. By that time, Austin had developed a less original undertone. If you were a gal between the ages of twelve and twenty, you felt the changes all too sharply.

In some ways, Austin became no different from other college towns with punk scenes and bands who were looking for "jailbait"—young teens who didn't understand yet that "No." was a complete sentence, and actually an option.

Today, I'm thankful for an ever-evolving language that makes it much easier to speak to these truths. There are many of us who survived the 1980s together, still lifting as we climb by supporting others in our communities and raising a new crop of good den mothers. May our nieces, daughters, and granddaughters all feel a sense of belonging, without ever becoming a statistic.

Ash at Home, September 1984.

Next: **Fang**, Liberty Lunch, Fall 1984.

WE SUCK
OF COURSE

FANG, LIBERTY LUNCH, FALL 1984.

Peavey

Flipper Crowd, Liberty Lunch, January 1985.

Facing: **Marching Plague**, Club Foot, August 1983.

Debbie Pastor, Winter 1987.

Facing: **Ralph Armstrong and Friend**, Thundercloud subs, Winter 1984.

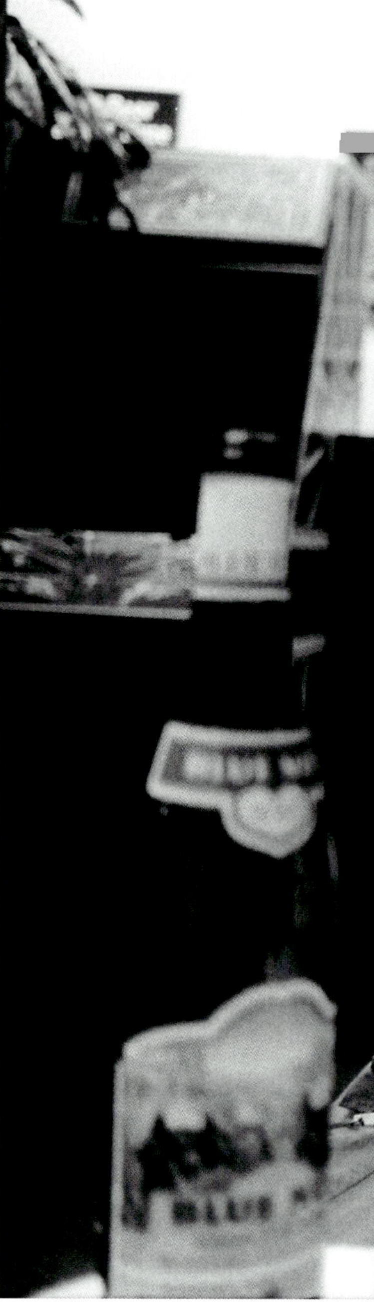

Karla Eppler, East 12th St., January 1985; **Tomas Levy and Friend**, East 12th St., January 1985.

Time Out, East 12th St., April 1985.

Party Guest, East 12th St., January 1985.

Facing: **"Sherri Baby" Canon** (left) and **Friend**, East 12th St., January 1985; **El Borracho Hits a High Note**, East 12th St., January 1985.

WHO CARES?

Consolation.
East 12th St., March 1985.

Rose Tattoo

(L–R) **Roger "El Borracho" Manriquez, Buddy Boy, Tommy Pipes, and Jerry Paterson**, April 1986.

Nick the Dick, East 12th St., March 1985; **Looking up a number**, convenience store, January 1985.

After the party, East 12th St., January 1985; **One A.M.**, Thundercloud Subs, Winter 1984.

"The redneck had a crowbar. I smashed a window in his car, but the guy hit Harry and myself, and we both went to the hospital. I ended up with an 'S'-shaped scar on my head. I had to learn the alphabet and how to read all over again. After that, I took a 'who cares?' attitude for twenty years." **–RICHARD "CROWBAR" MATHER**

RICHARD MATHER OF CRIMINAL CREW. ATOMIC CITY, WINTER 1985.
NEXT: **LYNDA STUART AND RENEE MILLER AT HOME**, FALL 1984.

Budweiser

LIFE ON THE LEDGE

BY DAVID YOW

THE HUNS WERE THE FIRST punk band I ever saw. That was Halloween 1979 at Raul's on Guadalupe Street in Austin. The experience changed my life forever. I was so taken by the idea that watching a band could be dangerous for the audience—and the band, too. At that time, slam dancing wasn't the sort of choreographed, testosterone nonsense it became later. Violence was generated among the crowd because the whole thing was so fucking exciting. Granted, there was pushing and shoving, cigarette flicking and beer cans flying around, but it was an exhilarating blast!

The Dicks were arguably the best and most rousing band ever to come out of Texas. They were intimidating and great—sloppy and wonderful and drunk and callous and fun. Their guitarist, Glen Taylor, was perpetually hammered, often barely able to stand, but he always had the most intoxicating, noisy guitar crap shooting out of whatever amplifier he borrowed. Pat "Bam Bam" Deason played the drums like he was trying to kill them. His face would be crunched into a tight wad of intensity with a cigarette butt clamped in the corner of his mouth. Buxf Parrot was like the American Sid Vicious without any of the glitz. He was menacing and irreverently smug, and his bass was a weapon. Gary Floyd, the singer of the Dicks, was brazen and truly formidable, a portly cross-dressed madhouse of a man. He was such a cool, mean nightmare to watch, but his growl had all the soulful rasp of Diana Ross. Motown was as important to the band's music as Hendrix, Creedence, and whatever punk rock they liked—but please keep in mind that the Dicks inspired much more punk rock than they ever took from it.

Some time in the fall of 1980, my best friend Steve and I were in his dorm room drinking beer in preparation for the Dicks show that night. Steve and I, and all our punk friends, were pretty well despised by the regular dumbass chumps who populated the gigantic dormitory. Those fuckers did a thing to

§§§§ **DAVID YOW**, MUFFY'S KITCHEN, FALL 1984.

us called "pennying in." If someone in the hallway put a bunch of pennies between the door and its metal frame, the door became impossible to open from inside the room. After the pennies were in place, one of these frat boy wannabes would dial the phone number of the victim's room. When the victim answered, their tormentor simply left the phone off the hook, rendering the victim's phone unusable and busy for the night because of how the dorm switchboard was set up.

The phone rang.

Steve answered, and then he immediately slammed down the receiver and slid the sliding volume control on his all-in-one hi-fi record player to full volume. Presto, we were *fucked*! Cell phones wouldn't be invented for quite some time yet. Until someone opened the dorm room door from the outside, we weren't going *anywhere*.

There we were, trapped on the fourth floor. Our cell was decorated with flyers for local shows, and a great big Sex Pistols poster with photos from their Winterland Ballroom show in 1978. Fortunately we had a case of beer. And we were blasting Fear, Circle Jerks, Black Flag, the Dicks, et cetera at a volume inspired by our imprisonment. Clearly we were *really* pissed off, but there was nothing we could do.

However, outside the building, a couple of feet below Steve's window was an exterior ledge all of about four inches wide. After a lot of courage-building beers, I got so fed up that I decided to brave this teeny ornamental ledge that the dorm's architect had thoughtfully provided. I figured I could flatten myself as much as possible against the exterior brick wall and inch my way along the perilous strip over to the window of the neighboring room, which, I'm guessing, was about fifteen feet away. Four stories up on that puny brick sill, the distance seemed a great deal larger. I *should* have been scared, but I wasn't.

I made it. At the next window, two diligent students were studying inside. They were understandably shocked when I pounded on the glass. I ordered them to open up and let me in. Their unexpected reply was, "Okay, but first, turn down the music!"

I couldn't fucking believe they were so concerned about the punk rock blasting on the other side of their wall that they would use it as a bartering tool while I was, quite literally, inches from death. Steve was poking his head out of his window behind me, and he had a crazy look on his face. I screamed back at him, "TURN IT DOWN!"

He did, and the two pricks let me climb into their room.

And the show? The Dicks were particularly great that night.

David Yow at Muffy's, Fall 1984.

Next: **Scratch Acid** (L–R: David Yow, Rey Washam, David Wm. Sims, and Brett Bradford), Spring 1986.

EXIT

Brett Bradford and **David Yow**,
Scratch Acid, closing night of
Voltaire's Basement, July 1984.

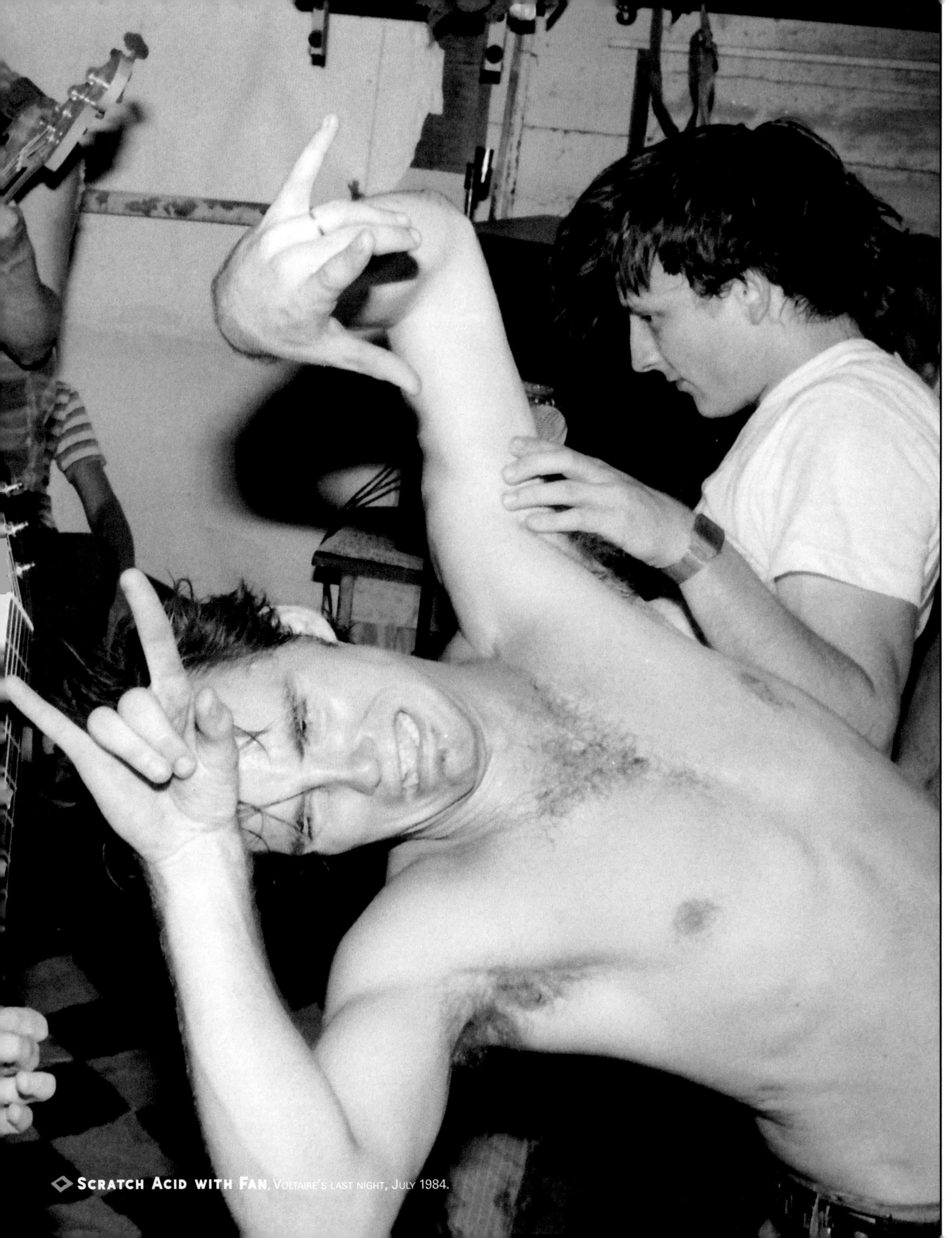

◇ **Scratch Acid with Fan**, Voltaire's last night, July 1984.

Brett Bradford and **David Yow**, Scratch Acid, Voltaire's last night, July 1984.

David Wm. Sims, David Yow, Brent Grulke, and Man in Vest
Scratch Acid, Uncle Sue Sue's, July 1984.

DAVID WM. SIMS, SCRATCH ACID, UNCLE SUE SUE'S, JULY 1984; **LISA KATHERINE "RALPH" ARMSTRONG, "TEXAS" TERRI LAIRD, AND DAVID WM. SIMS**, SCRATCH ACID SHOW, UNCLE SUE SUE'S, JULY 1984.

Rey Washam and **Brett Bradford of Scratch Acid**, Uncle Sue Sue's, July 1984.
Next: **David Yow of Scratch Acid**, Uncle Sue Sue's, July 1984.

Bill Anderson and Sally King, Fall 1984.

Gibby Haynes and Mark Farner, B.O.S.S. Studios, San Antonio, July 1984.

Me in the Van, Boston, Fall 1985; **After-party**, San Antonio, April 1984.

Mark Farner, B.O.S.S. Studios, San Antonio, July 1984; **Chris and Simon**, Halcyon Co-op, September 1982.

King Coffey, B.O.S.S. Studios, San Antonio, July 1984.
Facing: **Joe "King" Carrasco**, East Austin, July 1985.

Mike Carroll in His Room, with Confederate flag and Crass poster, Fall 1984.

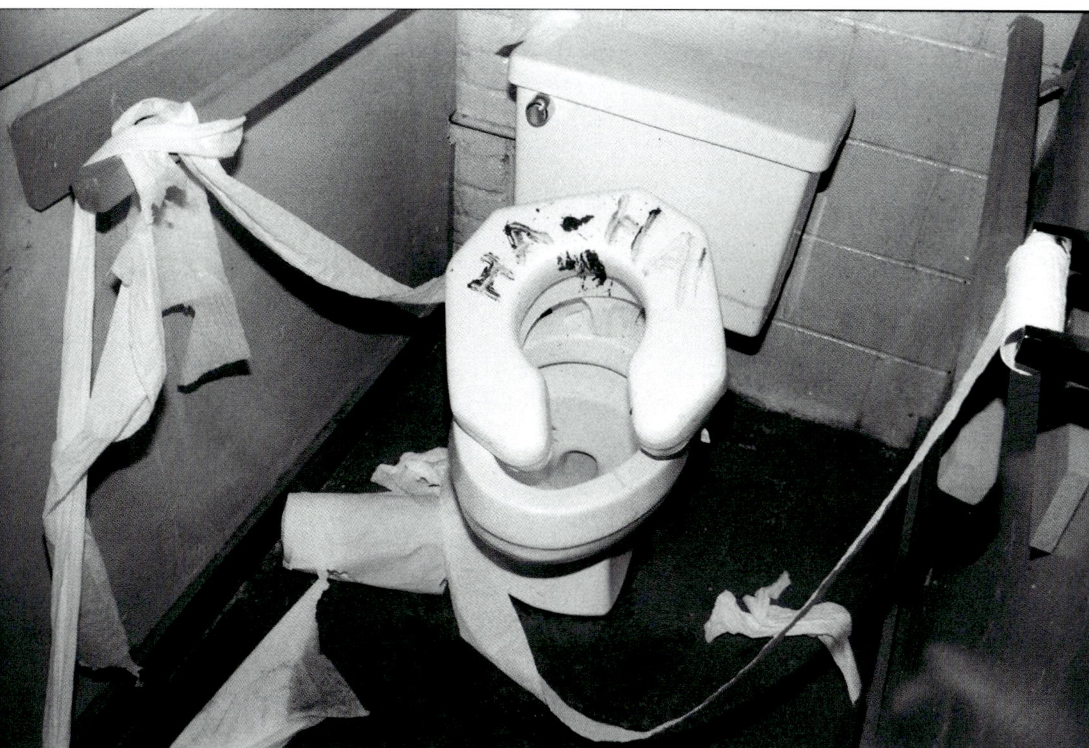

Backstage at a Buttholes show, 5th Street Theatre, September 1985.
Wind-powered turntable, Butthole house, Highway 183, Winter 1987.

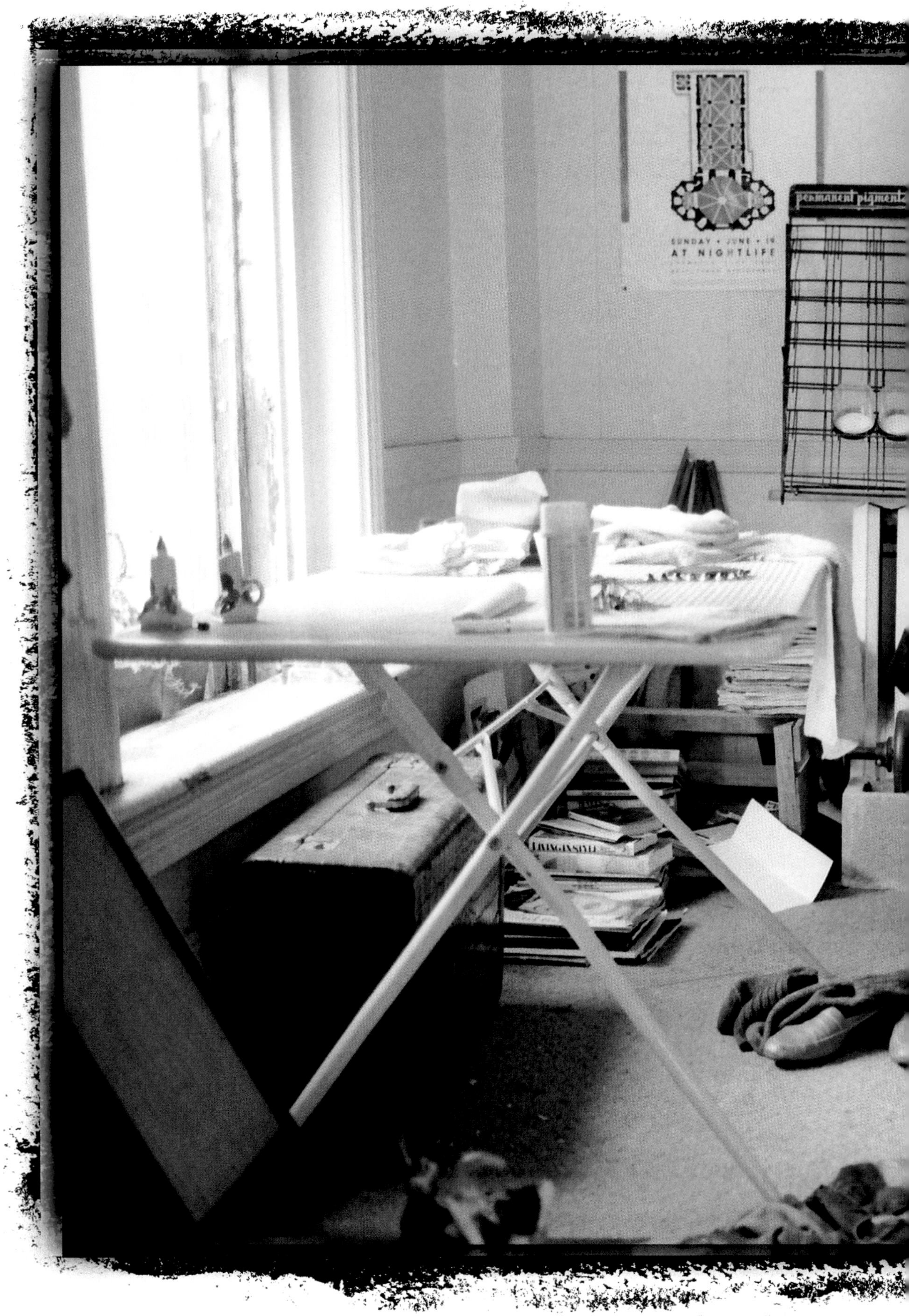
SUNDAY • JUNE • 19
AT NIGHTLIFE

John Hernandez, San Antonio, April 1984.

Richard "Curly" Cearley, Rollo's parlor, Winter 1985; **Ash gets a New Tattoo**, Winter 1985.

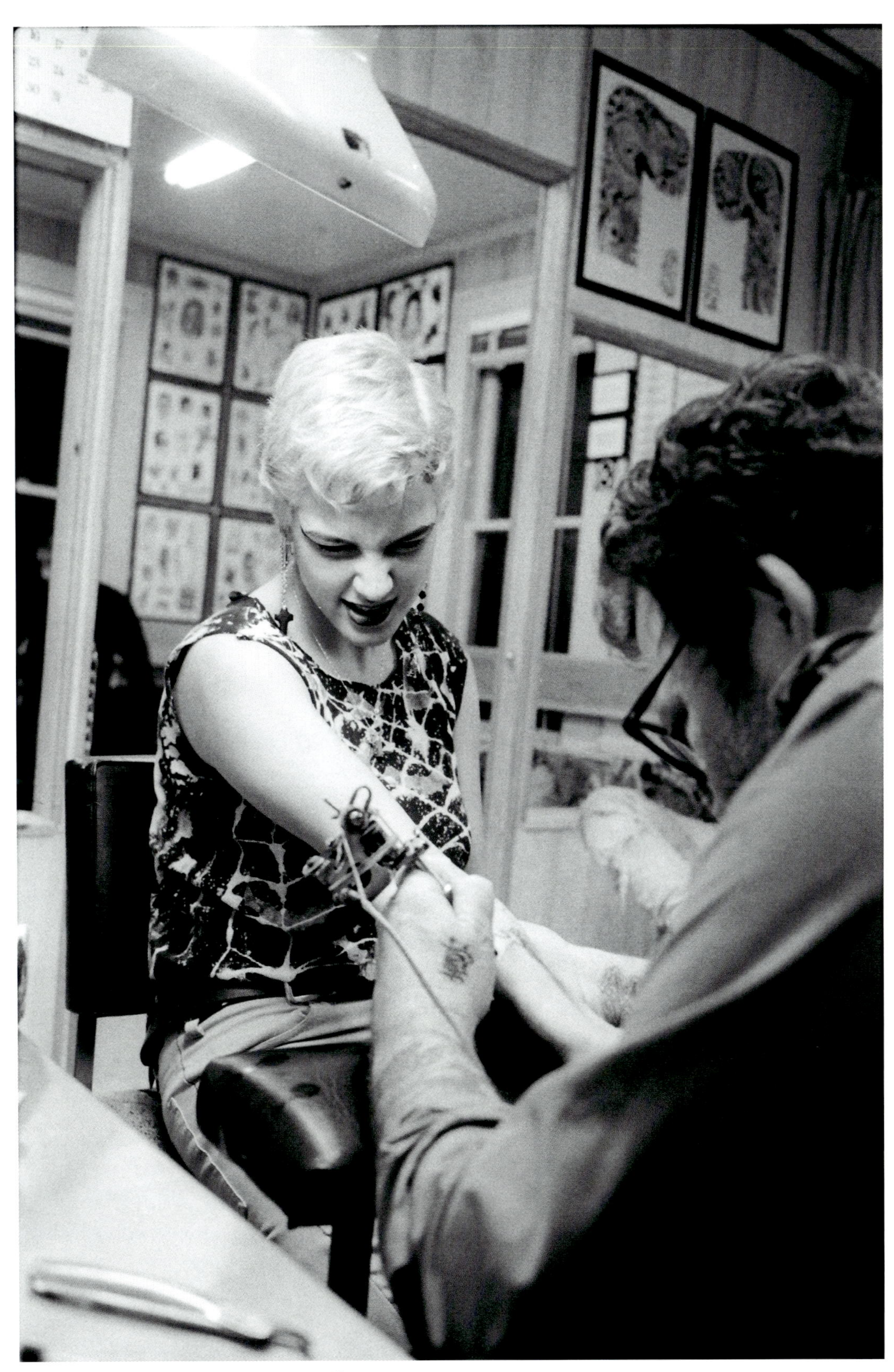

Ash and Mike "Rollo Banks" Malone, Winter 1985.

The Jeffersons, Voltaire's Basement, April 1984.

Facing: **Bufx Parrot of the Jeffersons** and **Santiago**, Voltaire's Basement, April 1984.

DANIEL JOHNSTON, TAPING OF MTV'S *THE CUTTING EDGE* SEGMENT ON THE "NEW SINCERITY" SCENE, JULY 1985.

Daniel Johnston with his Yip/Jump cassette, Sound Exchange, February 1986.

Steve Collier of Doctors' Mob, Liberty Lunch, January 18, 1986.

DOCTORS' MOB, WOODSHOCK, HURLBUT RANCH, JUNE 1985.

Glass Eye and **Barbecued meat**, Woodshock, June 1985.

Helen Moroney and Edmund "Edmo" Martinez, Woodshock, June 1985.

Next: (L–R) **Rat's Ass of Tales of Terror, Meredith, Capt. Trip of Tales of Terror,** and **Mara Beth "Dumplin'" Danger**, Woodshock, June 1985.

After: **Swimming hole**, Hurlbut Ranch, June 1985.

Maria Cotera, Woodshock, June 1985.

SOMEDAY ALL THE ADULTS WILL DIE!

PAT BLASHILL

THE MISFITS HAD NEVER been to Texas. They were just four lunkheads from Lodi, New Jersey, who had heard about punk. They wore black leather jackets and were obsessed with the Ramones and bad monster movies. Then in 1978, they recorded "Bullet," a pornographic punk rock classic driven by the lyric: "Texas is the reason/ That the President's dead." Why?

As he crooned, the group's singer, Glenn Danzig, seemed to be suggesting that John F. Kennedy was killed in Dallas in 1963 because of an inexorable American death drive—epitomized by the violent myth and reality of the Lone Star State.

Danzig would later prove to be a very unreliable narrator of the American experience, but in this case, he was onto something. In the late 1970s, a sacrilegious horde of great punk bands began to lurch and scuttle out of Austin, San Antonio, Houston, and Dallas. Renegade Texan fanzine editors and filmmakers lobbed bombs at the regional status quo. Many of these people were merely carrying out the prime directive of youth—it's fun to piss off your parents. But most of us were responding to local conditions: stultifying conservatism, virulent racism, and the hypocrisy of born-again Christianity.

Then as now, Texas was fascinating, exotic, repulsive and unbelievable, especially to people who didn't live there. Author Lawrence Wright has written that "Texans see themselves as a distillation of the best qualities of America: friendly, confident, hardworking, patriotic, neurosis-free. Outsiders see us as the nation's id, a place where rambunctious and disavowed impulses run wild."

Texas is still the most American of places, and the most extreme American place. It's the pride and embarrassment of the nation. Many citizens may not have ever heard the words "Texas" and "punk rock" in the same sentence. When they do, it makes perfect sense. Texas is the reason.

Few of us would have said as much back in the day. Next to other, blonder Texans, we were just losers, fags, and wolves who looked so sick in the sun. We were discovering who we were by making

DANCER, The Ritz Theater, Austin, Summer 1984.

weird music, style, and culture in a place where we had to do it for ourselves. In Austin, the Big Boys ended their shows by telling the audience, "Okay, now go start your own band!" Instead, I started bringing my camera to shows, and I tried to photograph everything.

We loved the Butthole Surfers because they pushed way beyond acceptable standards of noise, beauty, and personal hygiene. I was very taken with the fear and humor in their music. On the other hand, I felt the hurt and betrayal in the Dicks song, "Saturday Night at the Bookstore." When Scratch Acid released their first EP, I was stunned. How had a group which included one of the goofiest humans I had ever known made such a piece of important *art*? Did I feel that way because I wanted to make art, too?

We learned how to be part of something larger than ourselves. It was a kind of formation. We gave ourselves permission to act out, to behave badly, and to define "good" differently. But when a group of people learn they can throw away almost everything their parents and neighbors had taught them, what do they have left?

This is how four of us answered that question. For me, it started with a black satin Cheap Trick baseball jacket. I bought it for twenty bucks at Custom Records in Highland Mall in Austin in 1979 at the same store where I had bought the first two Cheap Trick records. Although I read about punk rock in *Creem* magazine, I hadn't heard any actual punk music. So when I heard Cheap Trick, I thought, "Maybe this is punk rock?" It sounded so urgent—raw but brightly melodic, brutal and sort of...odd.

Growing up way out north in suburban Austin, I avoided Little League baseball and bought fifty-cent records in a flea market called Pirate's Den. I was a bookworm who became a stoner, then a drama fag, then a stoner again. I worked at Baskin-Robbins 31 Flavors and a Swensen's ice cream store. Then I got a job as an usher at the Village Cinema Four. One day, I wore my Cheap Trick jacket to work.

During the breaks between movie screenings, we cleaned up the popcorn and empty paper cups beneath the seats. That day, I was working with the new guy, a shy kid named Steve. I was scraping a Twizzler off the floor, and I almost jumped when Steve spoke.

"Hey, uh, that's a pretty cool jacket."

"Oh, thanks."

"Do you like Cheap Trick?"

"Yeah. They're pretty cool."

This was our entire first conversation. But in the weeks afterwards, we started talking about music. Sometimes when we took our breaks, we'd sit in Steve's purple Camaro and listen to the Cars or Devo. "Check out this guitar solo: the guy plays for a little bit, then he stops, then he starts again, then he stops again. It's really weird."

As it happened, Devo had already wrecked Steve's life. He was from West Austin, which seemed straighter and a bit more affluent than my neighborhood. Steve played in the school band, but he was also a skateboarder. When he saw Devo on *Saturday Night Live*, he thought they must be a novelty act. Who could take those robot moves and synthesizer riffs seriously? But he kept listening to their tape, until one day, they just sounded great. That night, he called his girlfriend, Kelly, who was a classically trained pianist.

"You know, it's weird, but I really like this Devo album."

Kelly started crying. New wave had ruined her boyfriend forever.

In the fall of 1979, Steve and I started classes at the University of Texas. One night, we were loitering outside of Theater 3 when Steve mentioned a bar on the Drag, a strip of shops across from the UT campus. He said, "My band is playing there Tuesday night."

"Really?"

"Yeah, you should come see us."

"What's your band called again?"

"The Big Boys."

Raul's had once been a Mexican American music club, but now they booked different sorts of bands. The carpets were permanently sticky, and one wall was covered with a giant mural of two rats perched at the edge of a sewer pipe. When I got there, the guy at the door looked like a biker, but he didn't ask for ID—which was all I cared about since I was still seventeen.

The Big Boys were already playing, although they kept introducing themselves as Kaye Mart and the Shoppers. The singer, the bass player, and the guitarist actually were *big boys*. Wearing dresses. So was Steve—plus mascara.

The Big Boys made a jagged, primitive sound that had something funky underneath. The singer, who called himself Biscuit, introduced one song as "Mutant Rock." "When the world is blown away, and mutants are the thing," he sang, "...mutant rock will be the rage and it will sweep the land."

Raul's wasn't crowded. Some of the girls were wearing sleeveless British flag T-shirts or spiky hair, and some of the guys were sporting sunglasses, but the scene was mostly dark and shabby. This didn't look like the punk rock I had seen on TV, but everyone did seem really creative. I started taking pictures.

I had entered a complete, self-sustaining world. Every band was doing their own songs. The audience was full of characters—like Sarita Crocker and Clair LaVaye, who were said to be witches and supposedly slept in coffins. Over the next few months, I became a regular. I would stand up front, close to the band. When they finished playing—if I liked them—I'd lean in and say, "You guys were good!" And they would say, "Thanks."

As a teenager, I had seen lots of touring bands in huge concert halls. At Raul's, I discovered that transcendent music is sometimes made by actual humans. Humans you can speak to. After you understand that, you don't need rock stars anymore.

When I first saw Stella floating through a nightclub, she was wearing rosary beads and long black gloves. She seemed impossibly glamorous, like a doomed Weimar princess. But she grew up in the Metroplex, otherwise known as the agglomerated disasters of Dallas and Fort Worth. It's one of the ugliest places on Earth, with churches that look like shopping malls, and schools that look like prisons. Her name was Lisa then.

When Stella moved to Austin and into a student dormitory, she was a goody-goody. A lot of the young ladies in the dorm were joining sororities; she could have done that too, and her parents would have been so proud. UT sororities were the first step towards an upstanding heterosexual life. If you got into a good house, you would have a very good chance of meeting a boy from a very good family, going to really great parties and just having a lot of fun in Austin!

But Stella didn't want to bag a husband and have a bunch of brats in a suburban home. She had been to Europe. She looked at French and Italian *Vogue*. She liked the movie *Cabaret*. She liked the new wave music Texas radio DJs were starting to slip in between REO Speedwagon and Pink Floyd. Still, "I didn't feel confident enough to do my own thing," she says.

Eventually, someone talked her into going to see the Go-Go's at Club Foot. Stella had heard their songs on the radio. She hadn't heard of the Big Boys, who were opening. She'd definitely never seen a huge guy in drag singing for a band. It was startling, and she enjoyed it very much. The Go-Go's were okay too.

Stella went back to Club Foot to see Billy Idol and X. The drinks weren't too expensive, and the people were friendly enough. She even went by herself sometimes.

Monday through Friday, she kept her grades up, and stuck with her declared major, Radio-Television-Film. Then Stella ended up in an advertising class with Chris Gates, the bass player for the Big Boys. He looked scary, but Stella soon decided he was a teddy bear. He became part of her new circle of friends.

Chris told Stella about Gang of Four and the Cure. She became a devoted fan of both bands. When the Cure released their overwrought 1982 album, *Pornography*, Stella clutched it to her breast and never let go. She was talking up *Pornography* with her classmates one day when they were leaving class, and a music critic for the student newspaper began explaining to her why *Pornography* didn't stand up to the band's earlier work.

"Oh my god, what is wrong with you?!" Stella said. "It is clearly their masterpiece."

On the cover of that album, the Cure are a blur of pancake makeup and fright wigs. Within months, Stella started wearing her mascara a little thicker.

"A lot of us came from other parts of Texas, or had small, repressive upbringings," Stella says now. "For us, Austin was permission to let your freak flag fly."

On the other hand, Diane was only fifteen when she asked her father to drive her down the Drag as slowly as possible. She was glued to the window, staring at a couple of kids with Mohawks. She seemed to be taking notes, doing research. "Dad!" she squeaked. "Slow down!"

She had never liked sunny pop music. She didn't feel sunny. She loved David Bowie and Brian Eno, probably because the world they sang about was weird and fragile and beautiful. She loved Roxy Music. Roxy Music was like nothing she'd ever heard on the radio. They were very European, super sexy, and possibly insane. They were everything that South Austin was not.

She thought punk was disgusting at first. Then she decided it was the best thing in the world. Punk told her darker stories. Her best friend Kathy bought her records at garage sales. When she went over to Kathy's house, Kathy's mom would answer the door, take one look at Diane, and say, "Oh, you girls. It's Halloween every day with you two."

Kathy started calling herself Ralph. She told Diane about the punk rock shows happening on the UT campus. One night, just after she turned sixteen, Diane climbed out of her bedroom window and went to her first punk show at an off-campus dorm called New Guild. When she got there, Diane wandered around the scuffed-up old mansion. Someone gave her vodka.

By the time the Dicks started playing, Diane was potted. They started with a broken glass riff that seemed slightly out of the band's control. "Daddy, daddy, daddy—proud of his son!" howled singer Gary Floyd. "He's got him a good job—kills niggers and Mexicans!" This was "Hate the Police," the band's one minute-and-fifty-nine-second magnum opus.

Diane loved this singer in a Mao tunic,

and she loved the Dicks. She loved the audience. She thought, "These are people I want to get to know and spend time with. These are *my people*."

A few weeks later, Diane saw a poster on a light pole on the Drag. The art was a cartoon of a frat boy and a sorority girl, decorated with arrows and helpful captions like, "Too much makeup," "Mexican peasant dress," and "Straw bag full of credit cards." At the top were the words: HOW TO RECOGNIZE THE ENEMY!

Diane went home and gathered all her preppy clothes. She tore them apart, then put them back together again. She found a Neiman Marcus purse that she could swing. She had completed her research. She would be the purest white girl in Hell. She would call herself "Muffy."

I met Muffy later, when my friend David Yow was sleeping on her couch. I dropped by her place one night. According to Muffy, I was instantly besotted with her pal, the infamous Becky Balboa. Muffy was in a feisty mood. She was pretty sure she was about to be fired from her job as a cook at a popular bakery. She improvised a raiding party. I was roped into the scheme as getaway driver.

Muffy, Yow, and the vaguely thuggish MacDonald brothers piled into my mom's Cutlass Supreme, and I carted us all to the bakery. They told me they were picking up some "work clothes," and that they would only need a second. They returned with several bottles of champagne and enough food for a week. I asked no questions and deposited them neatly back at Muffy's place. I am told I was very jolly, which is strange, because I know I would have been unhappy breaking the law.

In the beginning, back in A.D. 1979, two laws were immutable: everything old was bad, and rock stars were worse. The Huns, possibly the most infamous Raul's band, sang a song called "Glad He's Dead." It was about JFK.

The laws started changing a few years later, after Steve quit the Big Boys. It was no longer fatal to admit that you liked country and western music, Frank Sinatra, or Black Sabbath. David Yow's band Scratch Acid even played a song from *Jesus Christ Superstar*.

In any case, *everybody* was psyched to see the Misfits play at the Ritz in 1982—and not just because they played guitars made out of bones. Steve loved the Misfits, especially their song about 1960s horror movie host and Ed Wood starlet Vampira.

At the Ritz the night of the show, Steve climbed up to the balcony. He didn't know that the balcony was also the backstage area. He saw the boys in Crotch Rot smoking pot with a couple of Misfits. He saw about eight cans of Aqua Net hair spray lined up in front of a mirror. Then Glenn Danzig walked in. He was such a short fellow!

Danzig walked over to the mirror, grabbed a huge forelock of his blue-black hair, and pulled it down in front of his face. Then he began to empty one of the cans of Aqua Net into his hair until the forelock was a hardened, lethal point. Steve was transfixed.

Three hours later, the show had already entered Austin legend as the loudest punk rock show *ever*. The Misfits were cranked up so high that they shook big chunks of plaster off the ceiling of the theater. Muffy, who was a die-hard fan, escaped, and she spent most of the show out on Sixth Street, like everyone else.

I wasn't there, and by the next morning I knew I had fucked up. That week, I scrambled around asking everyone, "How were the Misfits?!" They all said the same thing: "They were horrible! They were just like Kiss!"

Finally I got to Steve.

"How were the Misfits?!"

"They were *great*!" he said. "They were *just like Kiss*!"

Afterward, Steve embraced all the music he'd always loved—from the Who to the Ramones—and baked it into a drunken, frequently hilarious post-punk mess called Doctors' Mob. They enjoyed a moment of fame when MTV came to town in 1985 to document the Austin scene. Steve later became a successful animator for clients including the University of Texas football team.

Stella soon tired of her role as an unapproachable muse. She got a less severe haircut, and joined an idiosyncratic rock band called Glass Eye. She toyed with the idea of moving to New York or Los Angeles, but eventually realized she wanted to stay within two miles of UT, which she still regards as the mother ship.

Muffy reverted back to Diane, but continued to cook. She moved to Minneapolis, and married one of the Cherubs, an excellent Texas noise rock band influenced by the Butthole Surfers. She too returned to Austin. David Yow still calls her Muffy.

Gradually, I learned how to take better punk rock photographs. In 1985, I got into tour vans to travel with Doctors' Mob and Glass Eye. I was a lousy roadie, but I had a great time. After that, I never really came back to Austin.

A couple of days before I left Texas for good, I saw Bill Anderson, the guitar player for Poison 13. Bill was handsome and tough, and he put a sharp, cutting edge on everything he said. That night, he grinned and told me, "If it doesn't work out in New York, just come back here and no one will give you a hard time."

Was that reassurance, or a dare?

I just said, "Thanks, Bill."

Big Boys crowd, the Ritz, July 1982.

Dead Kennedys, the Ritz Theater, August 1982.

Facing and next: **Devo**, Armadillo World Headquarters, August 2, 1979.

Meat Puppets, Continental Club, February 1985.

Facing: **Glenn Danzig**, Liberty Lunch, September 1984; **Eerie Von** of **Samhain** Liberty Lunch, September 1984

Next: **Samhain**, Continental Club, December 1984.

Fender

FERRE

Above and next: **The Replacements**, Liberty Lunch, January 1985.

Facing: **Soul Asylum**, Continental Club, March 1986.

Sonic Youth, Continental Club, April 1986.

Roky Erickson, the Ritz Theater, February 1987.

Facing: **David Yow** of **Scratch Acid**, the Ritz, January 1985.

Next: **Paul Leary** and **Juan Molina of Butthole Surfers**, 5th Street Theatre, September 1985.

BUTTHO

Gibby, Butthole Surfer, the Ritz, January 1985.

Doing Gibby's hair, Butthole Surfers show, 5th Street Theatre, September 1985;
Gibby Haynes, Butthole Surfers, 5th Street Theatre, September 1985.

Gibby Haynes, Butthole Surfers, Club Foot, October 1983.

Next: **Gibby Haynes and Paul Leary**, Butthole Surfers, Club Foot, October 1983.

Randy "Biscuit" Turner, Final Big Boys show, Liberty Lunch, September 23, 1984.

Next: **Tim Kerr of the Big Boys**, July 1982.

Marshall

"Big Chris" Gates on the Big Boys Van, Winter 1984.

Facing: **Glass Eye Tour**, Fall 1985; **Steve Collier in the Lisa Marie**, Fall 1985.

◊ **Kathy McCarty of Glass Eye**, Minneapolis, Fall 1985.

Doctors' Mob, Washington Monument, Washington, D.C., Fall 1985.

Jesus on the Dash, Fall 1987.

Facing: **King Coffey**, Butthole Surfers, San Antonio, July 1984.

A TEXAS TRIP, 1963–2006

November 22, 1963	President John F. Kennedy is assassinated in Dallas. He is immediately succeeded by Vice President Lyndon B. Johnson, a Texan.
August 1, 1966	In Austin, ex-marine and Boy Scout leader Charles Whitman kills his mother and wife, then climbs to the twenty-eighth floor of the University of Texas Tower, where he opens fire on passersby across campus and along the Guadalupe Street Drag. He kills fourteen and injures thirty-one people before police shoot him dead.
November 4, 1967	Native son Roky Erickson sings for the Thirteenth Floor Elevators at the Vulcan Gas Company in downtown Austin. A poster advertising the show features Winnie the Pooh and his donkey companion Eeyore—the guest of honor at an annual Austin hippie festival called Eeyore's Birthday Party.
1969	Roky Erickson is arrested in Austin for possessing a single marijuana cigarette. To avoid prison, he pleads insanity and is sent to the first of several mental hospitals.
August 1970	Inner Sanctum Records opens in Austin, and becomes a countercultural hub for "cosmic cowboy" music.
1972	After enduring electric shock and Thorazine treatments, Roky Erickson is released from Rusk State Hospital. He forms a new band, which he calls "Bleib Alien." The name is a play on a German phrase meaning "stay alone."
January 3, 1976	PBS begins airing the live music show *Austin City Limits.* The debut broadcast features Asleep at the Wheel and the Texas Playboys.

April 23, 1976 *Ramones* by the Ramones is released. Meanwhile, Peter Frampton's *Frampton Comes Alive!* begins ten weeks at the top of the charts and becomes the best-selling album of 1976.

January 8, 1978 The Sex Pistols play Randy's Rodeo in San Antonio, Texas. Bystanders hurl hamburgers, beers, and pies at the band. Texas punks the Vamps open the show. Singer Frank Pugliese notes that Sid Vicious was "normal" but "weird," and that he stole a pair of sunglasses from the Vamps.

February 1978 Across from the UT Austin campus, a Tejano music club called Raul's hosts its first punk rock show: a double bill with the Violators and the Skunks. Raul's quickly becomes the nerve center of the local punk and new wave scene.

September 19, 1978 The singer of the Huns, Phil Tolstead, is arrested for obscenity while onstage at Raul's.

November 3, 1979 The Big Boys play their first show at a former fur coat storage facility known as the Vault.

Spring 1979 Inner Sanctum changes with the times and begins hosting in-store appearances and record release parties for local and touring bands including X, Squeeze, the Big Boys, Standing Waves, and Crotch Rot.

Spring 1980 Duke's Royal Coach Inn opens in the space once occupied by the Vulcan Gas Company. Duke's begins booking punk shows, including the first Austin gig of Nine Foot Worm Makes Own Food, aka the Butthole Surfers.

May 16, 1980 Legendary Austin concert hall Armadillo World Headquarters hosts the Punk Prom, with the Big Boys, the Next, Reactors, Sharon Tate's Baby and the debut performance of the Dicks.

November 4, 1980 Ronald Reagan becomes the fortieth President of the United States. That night, the Marxist U.K. band Gang of Four plays the new Club Foot in Austin. "We hear you've got a new president," sneers guitarist Andy Gill. "*Aren't you lucky?*"

December 19, 1980	The Big Boys and the Dicks split album *Recorded Live at Raul's Club* is released on Rat Race Records.
December 31, 1980	After a ten-year run, Austin's venerable music space Armadillo World Headquarters closes. The building is razed, and the land becomes a parking lot.
April 1, 1981	Raul's closes, following a magnificent three-year run of shows that helped spawn scores of Austin punk bands.
August 1, 1981	MTV begins broadcasting.
February 1982	Austin band the Stains moves to San Francisco and becomes M.D.C. Their first album, *Millions of Dead Cops*, includes the hit "John Wayne Was a Nazi."
Halloween 1982	Punk rock shows commence at the Skyline Club, a dance hall at the edge of Austin that opened in 1948 and previously hosted Hank Williams and Elvis Presley.
December 1, 1982	Quincy, the crusading NBC-TV medical examiner, confronts the evils of punk rock in an episode titled "Next Stop, Nowhere."
Spring 1983	The Dicks relocate to San Francisco. They spend April and May traveling and playing Rock Against Reagan shows with M.D.C., the Dead Kennedys, and others. After the tour, the majority of the band members return to Austin, while singer Gary Floyd stays in SF and recruits a new bunch of Dicks.
July 1983	The *Butthole Surfers* debut EP, aka *Brown Reason to Live* or *Pee Pee the Sailor*, is released on Alternative Tentacles.
1984	Young Daniel Johnston arrives in Austin with a carnival, then lands a job at a McDonald's near campus. He hands out cassettes of his anguished, lo-fi music on the street, telling people, "I'm Daniel Johnston, and I'm gonna be famous."
Winter 1984	A tiny UT campus bar called Uncle Sue Sue's—nestled on a side street next to several large fraternity houses—begins a fertile seven-month run hosting punk shows.

Spring 1984 Two of the Big Boys, guitarist Tim Kerr and bassist Chris Gates, spin off their psychobilly band Poison 13. Tensions increase within the Big Boys. Poison 13 do a few short U.S. tours and later emerge as a major influence on Seattle grunge bands such as Mudhoney and Pearl Jam.

July 1984 Scratch Acid records their debut EP for Rabid Cat Records, including the songs "Cannibal" and "Lay Screaming." Six years later, Kurt Cobain describes his band Nirvana as: "a Gang of Four and Scratch Acid rip-off."

August 20–23, 1984 The Big Boys and Dead Kennedys play sets during protests of the Republican National Convention in Dallas. On August 22, communist activist Gregory Lee Johnson burns a U.S. flag while chanting, "Ronald Reagan, killer of the hour, perfect example of U.S. power!" Johnson is arrested, convicted of a crime, and sentenced to one year in prison. His appeal goes to the U.S. Supreme Court, which rules in his favor, declaring his act is a form of protected speech.

September 23, 1984 After returning from a long tour, the Big Boys share a bill with Glenn Danzig's band Samhain at Austin venue Liberty Lunch. While playing, the Big Boys see a local Nazi recruiter handing out leaflets in the crowd. They call out the man, and fistfights erupt across the club. Shaken by the violence and frustrated with each other, the band collapses on the spot—this night turns out to be their last show.

February 1985 In the parking lot of a Mr. Gatti's chain pizza restaurant in Austin, a fight breaks out between a group of punks and rednecks. One of the latter attacks Criminal Crew bassist Richard Mather with a crowbar. Mather is hospitalized. When he recovers, friends begin calling him "Crowbar."

Spring 1985 First-wave Austin punk Jesse Sublett casually describes newer bands such as Glass Eye, the Reivers, Doctors' Mob, and True Believers as a form of "new sincerity," and the tag sticks all the way up to *Rolling Stone*. The movement finds an unlikely superstar when Glass Eye singer/guitarist Kathy McCarty becomes a champion of Daniel Johnston. His first-ever club gig is opening for Glass Eye at the Beach Cabaret.

June 29, 1985 The Woodshock '85 outdoor festival near Dripping Springs, Texas, features performances by Texas Instruments, Zeigeist, the Crybabys, the Offenders, and the Hickoids.

July 1985 The crew of MTV's *The Cutting Edge* arrives in Austin to document the music scene in the city. Daniel Johnston is not scheduled to appear in the program at all, but he charms his way into several scenes and steals the show.

September 20, 1985 The Butthole Surfers play a show in a downtown theater. Someone gives Daniel Johnston a hit of acid. He later writes a song about it: "I Did Acid with Caroline."

October 1985 *Spin*, a music magazine intended to be more daring competitor to *Rolling Stone*, publishes a review of Scratch Acid and a photograph by Pat Blashill. The writer calls their song "Mess" a "duet for rock band and shattered glass."

February 1986 The Butthole Surfers have been on the road almost continuously for two years. Drummer Teresa Taylor quits for a period, and the band adds a new member: a nude dancer and performance artist named Kathleen Lynch, also known as "Ta-Da the Shit Lady."

Summer 1986 Roland Swenson, ex-manager of local new wave group Standing Waves, enlists *The Austin Chronicle* editor Louis Black, *Chronicle* publisher Nick Barbaro, and booking agent Louis Meyers to organize a regional Austin music festival. They land on the name South by Southwest—or SXSW.

March 1987 The inaugural South by Southwest festival attracts more than seven hundred attendees, wildly exceeding expectations.

Summer 1991 The unthinkable occurs as the Butthole Surfers embrace the music business and sign with Capitol Records. Still, as guitarist Paul Leary tells *Details*, "Our music is like Jiffy Pop—more fun to make than it is to eat."

July 5, 1991 Richard Linklater's film *Slacker* opens in a national theatrical release. The critical success features many Austin musicians and local luminaries, including (now ex-)Butthole Surfers drummer Teresa Taylor, original

Scratch Acid singer Steve Anderson, and fanzine editor John "Control Rat X" Slate.

SUMMER 1993 Austin's Sound Exchange record store hires Daniel Johnston to paint a mural of his "Jeremiah the Innocent" frog on an exterior wall. Jeremiah had previously adorned the cover of Johnston's tape collection *Hi, How Are You?* Over a decade later, the record store is sold, and a fast food chain buys the building. They plan to destroy the mural, but Austin music lovers protest, and the frog is saved. The restaurant Thai, How Are You? later pops up in the space.

FEBRUARY 13, 1995 Drummer King Coffey of the Butthole Surfers spearheads a Roky Erickson revival by releasing an album of new Roky recordings, *All That May Do My Rhyme*.

1996 Guitarist Tim Kerr of the Big Boys and Poison 13 is inducted into the Texas Music Hall of Fame.

AUGUST 19, 2005 Randy J. "Biscuit" Turner, former singer of the Big Boys, dies in Austin.

DECEMBER 2006 Named after an anthemic Big Boys song, the Fun Fun Fun music festival begins a ten-year run as a celebration of punk, hip-hop, indie rock, and metal music. Stars of the first year's lineup include Circle Jerks, Spoon, Peaches, Quintron and Miss Pussycat, and Big Boys guitarist Tim Kerr's favorite punk band, the Riverboat Gamblers.

JANUARY 2011 John "John Boy" Hawkes of Meat Joy is nominated for an Academy Award for Best Supporting Actor for his role in *Winter's Bone*. His lengthy acting career, including roles in *Deadwood* and *The Sessions*, began in 1985 with the *Texas Chain Saw Massacre*-in-space slasher film *Future-Kill*.

Teresa Taylor's Terrific Top Ten

Ten Slabs of Texas Hot Wax by the Drummer Who Saw It All

MDC—Stains—"John Wayne Was a Nazi" 1981

When I first heard about punk, I went to local Austin record store Inner Sanctum, picked up the *NME*, and read all about English punk. I was converted on the spot. Afterwards, I had the most vivid dream of my whole life. In the dream, I saw myself putting the needle down on a 45, and it was "John Wayne Was a Nazi." I saw this giant, beautiful Indian chief standing over our suburban swimming pool. He cut himself, then dove into our pool. All the water was bloodred. When I woke up, I thought, "This is a racist country."

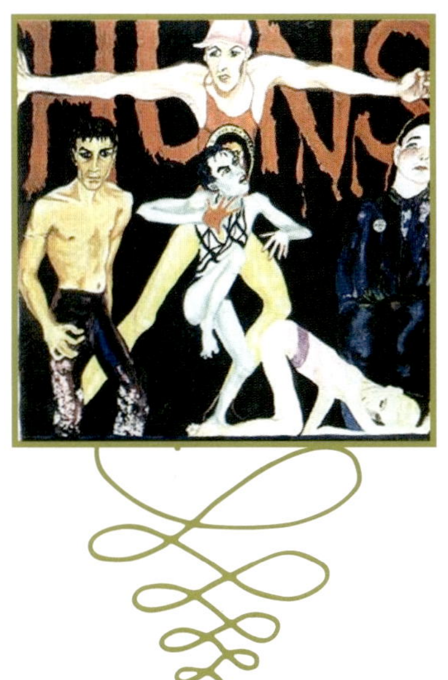

The Huns—"Glad He's Dead" 1979

I loved John F. Kennedy, and Jackie, and John John. I always had reverence for that family. So when the Huns sang, "I'm glad he's dead...I helped Lee Oswald shoot him in the head!!" it seemed sacrilegious. But I loved the fact that nothing was safe.

In 1991, I was in *Slacker*, talking about someone waving a gun around and shooting indiscriminately. Back then, that was something that people thought would only happen in Texas—not all the time, all over the world. People were scared of Texas. We were the real deal. We were inbred-looking hicks with thick accents!

◇ **Terence Smart** and **Teresa Taylor's Boots**, Butthole Surfers, the Ritz, January 1985.

The Offenders—"I Hate Myself" 1984

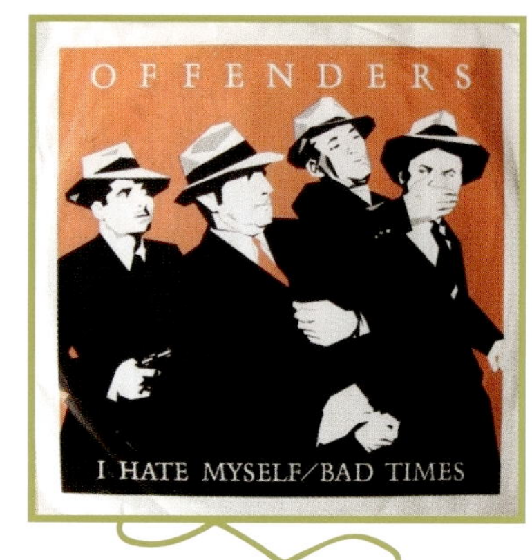

The Offenders were good at distilling really large ideas into one-liners. That was profound. With this song, I could not believe that someone had condensed everything I was starting to feel, everything I was going through, into that one line: "I hate...myself!!"

I was talking to their singer, JJ, one day outside of their practice space. He had shaved his head and his eyebrows. Then it started raining really heavily. JJ said, "Ahhh, shit!! I got water in my eyes!" I said, "That's why God gave you eyebrows."

The Delinquents—"Do You Have a Job for a Girl Like Me?" 1979

"Do you have something I can do on Thorazine?/ I smell bad and look strange and act really rude."

The lyrics of this song are the epitome of all of the reasons nobody would hire you, and every reason why that's not gonna work. These are some of the best lyrics I've ever heard. I can relate. It really took balls for some of us to go in and try to get jobs when our lifestyles were obviously on some *other* level. We were tripping on acid, and then going into convenience stores like U-Tote-M and asking if they were hiring. "Uhh...no."

Whoom-Elements—"Men in the Politics" 1982

Whoom-Elements bass player Diane Identity was the first person I met who was constantly thinking about how to hype her band. She had a girlfriend named Lisa X, who put an "X" on her forehead. I gave them rides home in my '66 Rambler convertible. They lived in a shack on Airport Boulevard. Lisa X huffed paint. When she told me about that, I said, "Oh honey, I can get you way better drugs than that."

DICKS—"HATE THE POLICE" 1980

Glen Taylor was one of the bluesiest hardcore punks you could ever have—he was a brilliant guitar player. It was the first time you could hear swampy blues thrown into the music, but the Dicks were punk as shit! Their posters were usually just pictures of big, hard penises.

Texas had the kind of gay men that people saw in *Deliverance*. Glen and his partner Santiago lived in a trailer park. Once my friend Dee and I went out there and climbed through their window. Dee and I were sitting there drinking all their beer when they came home. They didn't care, because they were already drinking beer, too. Glen said, "Oh, I'm glad you're here—did you fall through the window?"

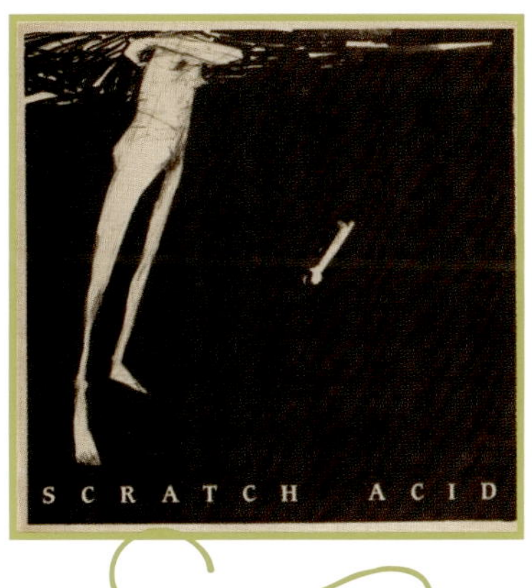

SCRATCH ACID—"CANNIBAL" 1984

Some of the lyrics in "Cannibal" are incredible. Rey Washam was the best drummer in the scene. David Yow was hi-larious. What a showman.

The Jackofficers, an offshoot of the Butthole Surfers, once played an infamous show at Voltaire's Basement. Our singer Gibby went to a theatrical prop store beforehand and got a Jack Daniel's whiskey bottle made out of hard sugar. Before the show, Gibby gave it to David Yow and said, "Make sure everyone sees you guzzling this Jack Daniel's, and act super drunk."

So he did, and then, at the peak of the show, Yow ran up and smashed the bottle over Gibby's head. Someone immediately turned around and punched David in the face. I think it was Roger, aka El Borracho, and he said, very sentimentally, "Don't do that to Gibby!" People took David to the ground and they were beating the shit out of him. They all thought they were defending Gibby, so it was touching.

Deborah Harry and Robert Jacks—
Der Einziger Weg (The Only Way) 1998

Austin punk singer and legend Robbie Jacks had played a cross-dressing Leatherface opposite Renée Zellweger in *Texas Chainsaw Massacre: The Next Generation*, and he was a huge fan of Debbie Harry from Blondie. He met her, and she just loved him. He went to New York City and stayed in her apartment, and they slept in the same big, luxurious bed with silk sheets.

When he told us the story, the room was full of lesbians who worshipped Debbie Harry. Robbie said that when Debbie got up, she was naked. "And I looked down," he said, "And I saw this shape." Then he made a pussy-shape with his three fingers.

All the dykes in the room said, "Yeah, yeah, that was her vagina!" Robbie said: 'Well, I'd never seen one before.' And all the dykes said, "Yeah, go on, tell us more!"

Debbie and Robbie adored each other. As a result, he had a chance to come up with some kind of hit song with her. Instead, he chose for them to record this loooong, slow bar song in German. Bad-ass!

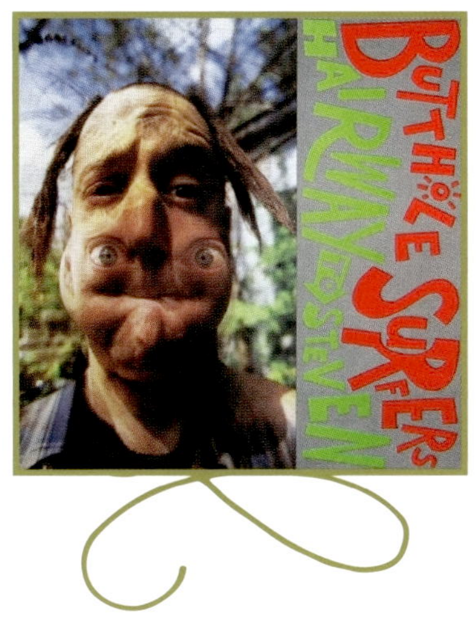

Butthole Surfers—Hairway to Steven 1988

This is my favorite Buttholes record. Paul Leary engineered everything. But Ric Wallace, who was our sound man for many years, also had a hand in *Hairway*. He was the only one who knew how to record my drums. A lot of other producers wanted to put me in a higher range, like a percussionist. But Ric said, "I'm gonna bring Teresa down, to the low—*boom boom!*—sound under King's drums. And it sounded fucking great. Tribal.

Big Boys—"Fun, Fun, Fun..." 1982

The Big Boys and the Dicks were polar opposites, but they defined themselves so clearly. I had so much fun slam dancing to this song, just bouncing from one person to another. I saw the Big Boys at the first Woodshock festival in 1981 at Waterloo Park downtown, and they had a whole horn section. We were so lucky, weren't we?

Acknowledgements

Thank you to the Big Boys, the Dicks, the Butthole Surfers, Scratch Acid, Poison 13, the Offenders, Doctors' Mob, Criminal Crew, Glass Eye, Meat Joy, Texas Instruments, Daniel Johnston, True Believers, Sonic Youth, Steve Shelley, Steve Collier, Stella Wier, Diane "Muffy" McGee Hardin, Tim Kerr, Lynda, Rene, Karla, John, Ralph, Roger, and everyone else who let me into their lives; to PhotoBill for showing me the way; to Gary Shove, for taking me seriously; to James Hannaham and Trace Crutchfield for rescuing me from the middle of the publishing mosh pit; to my excellent readers and editors RJ Smith, Gavin Edwards, Simon Reynolds, Michael Azerrad, Rich Malley and Jenny Huth; to my co-conspirators Rick, David, Donna, Ash and Teresa—you all killed it; to IAN, for meeting me on the mountain; to Adinah for sharing her trap favorites, to Vivi for dancing with me, and to Anette, for pretty much everything.

Rest in Peace to Randy "Biscuit" Turner, Chris Wing, Jukebox, Tony Johnson, JJ Jacobson, Mikey Donaldson, Brent Grulke, John Hernandez, Daniel Johnston, Mark "Chico" McCullough, Steve Anderson, Mike Carroll, Tommy Pipes, Dee Montgomery, Glen Taylor, Davy Jones, Tomas Levy, Jerry Paterson, Margaret Moser, Brian Hansen, Michael Malone, Roky Erickson, and Mark Farner.

Pardners

Richard Linklater is the Austin-based director of *Boyhood*, *Slacker*, and many other films.

David Yow is the singer for Scratch Acid, the Jesus Lizard, and Flipper. He plays important roles in the Netflix productions *I Don't Feel at Home in this World* and *Rattlesnake*. He lives in Los Angeles.

Adriane "Ash" Shown is an actor, artist, and playwright. She lives in Los Angeles.

Donna Rich is a psychotherapist. She plays a mean version of Elvis Costello's "This Year's Girl" on piano.

Teresa Taylor is a Butthole Surfer. She lives in Austin. Wednesday is her *South Park* day.

About the Photographer

Pat Blashill was born in Austin in 1961. He grew up listening to KNOW-AM radio as he fell asleep at night. The first record he bought with his own money was ZZ Top's *Tres Hombres*. He learned how to operate a 35mm camera in high school. After he saw photographs by Robert Frank, it was *on*.

Pat studied photojournalism at the University of Texas with Dennis Darling, J. B. Colson, and Ellen Wallenstein.

Inspired by punk bands at Raul's and local photographer Bill Daniel, he began shooting shows in 1980, and was pretty good by 1983. Pat took most of the photographs in this book with two cameras—a Canon TX and a Canon F-1—using a Vivitar 283 flash. He shot Kodak Tri-X black and white film, which he developed and printed himself.

In 1987, Pat left Texas for New York City, where he continued to photograph post-punk and indie bands. He began writing about music for magazines such as *Details*, *Spin*, and *Rolling Stone*. Little by little, he stopped taking pictures of musicians and their fans.

Pat moved to Vienna, Austria, in 2005, where he still lives with his wife and two daughters. He is an educator of refugees and an occasional pop critic. Pat still has the Canon F-1 and the Vivitar flash, and he uses them to photograph bands that float his boat.

"It was easy to keep your principles. Most didn't own much else."—**Jim "Straightedge" Koppenhaver**

The New Downtown Austin, February 1985.

Chris Gates's Jean Jacket, March 1985.

Next: **Mikey Milligan on a Frat Car** on the Drag, Spring 1985.

Front of book: **Criminal Crew** behind the Drag, F all 1984;

Title page: **Gibby Haynes** and **King Coffey**, Butthole Surfers, Club Foot, October 1983.

hastings